The
DOME
of the
ROCK

Oleg
Grabar

The Belknap Press
of Harvard University Press
Cambridge, Massachusetts
London, England
2006

D1202280

Library of Congress Cataloging-in-Publication Data

Grabar, Oleg.
   The Dome of the Rock / Oleg Grabar.
      p.   cm.
   Includes bibliographical references and index.
   ISBN-13: 978-0-674-02313-0 (alk. paper)
   ISBN-10: 0-674-02313-7 (alk. paper)
   1. Qubbat al-Sakhrah (Mosque : Jerusalem)   2. Architecture, Islamic—
Jerusalem.   3. Jerusalem—Buildings, structures, etc.   I. Title.

NA5978.J5Q334   2006
726′209569442—dc22   2006043560

The DOME of the ROCK

Preface

Some years ago I completed a book on early Islamic Jerusalem and contributed to a second book devoted more specifically to the Dome of the Rock. Both of these ventures were made possible by the stunning new photographs of the building's mosaics taken by Saïd Nuseibeh, along with an attempt by Dr. Muhammad al-Asad and Ms. Abeer Audeh to produce a computer generated reconstruction of the city before 1100. I thought at the time that these works signaled the end of my scholarly involvement with the Old City of Jerusalem, an involvement that began in 1953, when, as a finishing graduate student, I reached Jerusalem coming from the Jordan Valley and saw the Dome of the Rock for the first time. The time had now come, I thought, for new generations of scholars to pose new questions about this extraordinary building or to find new answers to old questions.

If, however, I return once again to the Dome of the Rock, it is for two reasons. One is the gentle persuasion of Margaretta Fulton, the distinguished and recently retired General Editor for the Humanities at Harvard University Press, who suggested that I write a book for a wide public about a masterpiece of world architecture. There was something appealing about writing without footnotes—merely telling the story of a striking building as I learned, felt, and understood it over more than half a century of acquaintance, and thinking of it as a work of art with a history amidst other architectural jewels rather than as a holy place in the Holy Land (although, as will become apparent, holiness and architectural quality cannot easily be separated from each other).

But the other reason to reconsider my self-imposed exile from the Dome the Rock was that, however much I had written on Jerusalem and on the Dome of the Rock over five decades, I knew that I had not succeeded in telling what the building meant in its long history and what it can mean today as a work of art, as an object for aesthetic feelings, not simply as a document for history emerging from hundreds of archaeological fragments and textual accounts, nor as a product of specific Late Antique consideration. It is also true that during the past decade, more or less since the completion of my earlier work, dozens of studies have appeared dealing with the Dome of the Rock, and several doctoral dissertations have concentrated on aspects of its history or its origins. Some of these new investigations are wonderful scholarly achievements, some others are important but not very interesting to read, and some are irritatingly incorrect; but all of them have illustrated something of the value and importance of the Dome of the Rock. Thus, yet another attempt to deal with the building may be worthwhile to explain its function or functions, the reasons for its visual power, and especially the unique relationship between a building that remained more or less unchanged and a political as well as spiritual history that changed a great deal over the centuries.

It is difficult to separate the story of a unique building from that of the unique city in which it is found. And I am not sure that, in the body of the text or in the Bibliography that accompanies it, I have always succeeded in differentiating between the two. But then neither did the written sources that deal with the Dome of the Rock. This is why I have emphasized inscriptions on the monument itself, rather than statements about it by chroniclers or travelers, which often have a different agenda from that of explaining the building. In looking at works of architecture, we are not accustomed to read, nor even to notice, the words that have been put on them. In fact, we do not even know whether they were ever noticed and studied as profoundly as were the sculptures on the facades of Gothic churches or those in the very fabric of Hindu architecture or the images found on the mosaics and paintings of Byzantine and Buddhist art. But it is reasonable to assume that the care exercised in the content of the inscriptions excludes their interpretation as merely decorative, however ornamental they are. Political power and religious or political ideology were expressed through inscriptions, and their meaning within their immediate contexts can be ferreted out more accurately than through texts that were often written elsewhere and, perhaps with a few exceptions, without the immediacy of the monument.

In short, this book is an attempt to make the building speak in the several successive dialects it employed: construction, decoration, architectural or urban setting, inscriptions on the building, and accounts of the building. To harmonize all these dialects is a difficult task, not less so since we lack, for the first nine hundred years of the building's history, the trivial documents that deal with expenses, requests by sponsors or artisans, orders for materials, and so on. These housekeeping records exist for the Ottoman period, from the sixteenth century onward. They provide a vivid picture of constant activities around the Dome of the Rock, but, as far as I have been able to judge, they fail to convey much about the building's effectiveness. But other scholars may feel differently, especially after all these documents have been properly analyzed.

And, finally, many new discoveries require monographs and learned discussions in order to be fully understood within the context of the Dome of the Rock. These include the fascinating church of the Kathisma of the Virgin recently uncovered near Jerusalem, which poses anew the problem of octagonal churches in Palestine, the endless details being discovered in medieval books of praises of Jerusalem, and our whole conception of Ottoman culture and ideology. I must acknowledge my limitations in dealing with these subjects and hope through this book to attract others to take them up.

Some practical remarks. The rocky outcrop under the Dome of the Rock will always be capitalized as the Rock. I shall refer to the vast surrounding man-made space as the Haram, short for al-Haram al-Sharif, the Noble Sanctuary, a name it acquired in Ottoman times. Generically, I will call this larger space the esplanade, and the smaller raised area on which the Dome of the Rock stands I will call the platform. Transliterations from Arabic have been simplified. Major Qur'anic inscriptions are presented in italic type, with clarifications of meaning and occasional early intrusions within the holy text in roman type. The Bibliography lists the primary as well as secondary sources I have used, arranged by chapter.

It remains for me to thank those who have helped in the completion of this book. Peg Fulton and Saïd Nuseibeh, whose photographs accompany the text, have been mentioned. Terry Grabar, Hana Taragan, Mika Natif, Patricia Crone, Michael Cook, and Slobodan Curcic have commented on or read parts of the text, answered occasional queries, and helped direct my thoughts. Jeffrey Spurr of the Fine Arts Library at Harvard University was, as ever, generous with his time and helpful. Susan Wallace Boehmer managed to make it all presentable in clear fashion, in spite of my continuing obfuscations. But my special thanks go to the keepers of the Dome of the Rock, the officials in charge of the endowment (the *awqaf*) of the Haram al-Sharif. Over the years Adnan al-Husaini, Issam Awwad, Yusuf Natsheh, and Khader Salameh were always welcoming and always helpful as I asked to see areas that were not always accessible to all and to chat about the problems of maintaining such a space. And I do want to thank, even though I can no longer recall their names, the Egyptian engineers in charge of restoration in 1960 and 1961, who, in difficult political times, allowed me to roam through a building being redone.

Contents

The DOME of the ROCK

Introduction

The Dome of the Rock is a beautiful Muslim shrine in the walled Old City of Jerusalem (Fig. 1). It consists of two sections imbricated into each other. The first is a tall cylinder (20 meters in diameter and 25 meters high) set over a large natural rocky outcrop, topped nowadays by a gilded dome made of aluminum alloy. The second is an octagonal ring (about 48 meters in diameter) of two ambulatories on piers and columns around the central rock (Fig. 2). The building is lavishly decorated both inside and outside. The interior displays artfully composed panels of veined marble, an astounding variety of mosaic compositions (primarily Arabic writing and vegetal motifs), gilt wooden beams, and a ceiling of leather embossed with ornament (Fig. 3). On the exterior are additional marble panels and a spectacular array of faience tiles with writing as well as vegetal or geometric ornament (Fig. 4).

Nearly everything one sees in this marvelous building, both inside and outside, was put there in the second half of the twentieth century. Tiles, mosaics, ceilings, and walls were redone during the course of several major overhauls carried out since 1958. These

1. The esplanade and platform of the Haram al-Sharif with the Dome of the Rock in the center as seen from the air. The greenery on the northern side (to the right) is recent. (Jon Arnold Images / Alamy.)

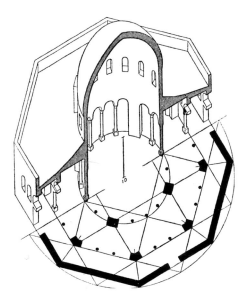

2. Schematic plan and section of the Dome of the Rock. (K. A. C. Creswell; Ashmolean Museum, Oxford.)

modern restorations were required, for the most part, to address structural damage from rain, frost, and earthquakes, from human incursions (relatively rare in recent centuries except for the illicit gathering of souvenirs), and from the natural aging of materials. All restorations claim to reflect the original state of the building in the last decade of the seventh century CE or, if the original state is unknown, to the earliest date that could be documented. However successful these restorations may have been, they lead us to the first paradox involving the Dome of the Rock: the assumption, by the Muslim faithful but also by many historians, that this building is a work of Umayyad art completed in 691 (the date provided by

3. General view of the interior, looking southward. (Saïd Nuseibeh.)

an inscription inside the building) under the sponsorship of the caliph (commander of the faithful) Abd al-Malik ibn Marwan, a prominent member of the first dynasty to rule the whole realm of Islam. In fact, as it stands, the building is almost entirely the work of our own times.

The Dome of the Rock is located on a more or less rectangular raised platform (north side: 156 meters; west side: 167.7 meters; south side: 128.1 meters; east side: 161.6 meters) to which access is

4. Exterior viewed from the south. Only the central part of the entrance block reflects its earliest stage. (Charles Bowman / Alamy.)

provided by eight sets of irregularly located stairs. The stairs are crowned by arcades that form a sort of bejeweled ring around the central building (Fig. 5). The platform itself is situated on a much larger and equally irregular rectangular esplanade (north side: 310 meters; west side: 488.3 meters; south side: 281.2 meters; east side: 466.6 meters) known to Muslims as the Haram al-Sharif (the Noble Sanctuary) and to Jews as the Temple Mount. It was cut out of the rock at the esplanade's northwestern corner and raised above a deep valley on the south side, with eastern and western outer walls adjusted to the sloping terrain. Access to this esplanade was provided by fourteen gates, three of which (to the south and east) have been blocked since time immemorial.

And with this esplanade we encounter the second paradox of the Dome of the Rock. The building, conceived as a nearly perfect geometric form, is not in the center of any part of the spaces on which it is built, and the two platforms are ill-fitted to each other (Fig. 6). Neither their dimensions nor their shapes seem interdependent, as would be expected from their location and from the assumed time (Antique and Late Antique) of their design. There does not seem to be any symmetry or observable visual sequence in the location of the gates to the esplanade. And, except for one, even the stairs leading up to the platform are not aligned with the esplanade's gates. It is as though different purposes and different rhythms lay behind each one of the components of the spatial environment of the Dome of the Rock.

The third paradox is more difficult to enunciate, and perhaps to grasp. It arises from the associations made with this space and the apparent contradictions involved in these associations. Thus, while scholars generally agree that Herod the Great (37 BCE–4 BCE) created a vast esplanade on top of Mount Moriah for his magnificent Second Jewish Temple, they do not agree about the original size of the Herodian space or about the location of such elements of the Temple as can be reconstituted from written sources—for instance, the Holy of Holies where the Ark of the Covenant was kept. More awkwardly, the function of the Dome of the Rock at the time of its construction in the late seventh century is uncertain. Over past centuries, the building has often been called the Mosque of Omar in non-Muslim accounts, even though neither the seventh-century caliph 'Umar nor any other 'Umar had anything to do with this structure, and it is certainly not a mosque. Several hypotheses attempt to explain what the Dome of the Rock was meant to be at the time of its creation, but only in the eleventh century was an association firmly established between the building and its most consistent popularly accepted purpose, repeated by tourist guides and pious books ever since: the commemoration of the Prophet Muhammad's mystical Night Journey to Jerusalem, followed by his Ascension through the heavens to contemplate the divine universe.

In spite of, or perhaps because of, these paradoxes, the visual attraction and spiritual power of the Dome of the Rock have been considerable, even though the expansion of the city of Jerusalem in every direction, except for the south, has weakened the building's immediacy within its urban context. Whether coming to Jerusalem from the east or from the south, a traveler first sees the almost antiseptically clean gilt cupola of the Dome of the Rock dominating a

5. Exterior viewed from the north. The arcade is later than the building and was part of a fancy ring surrounding the platform. (Erich Lessing / Art Resource, NY.)

6. The Haram al-Sharif today, with the large Aqsa Mosque to the south and a variety of buildings from many periods scattered around. (From Rosovsky, *City of the Great King.*)

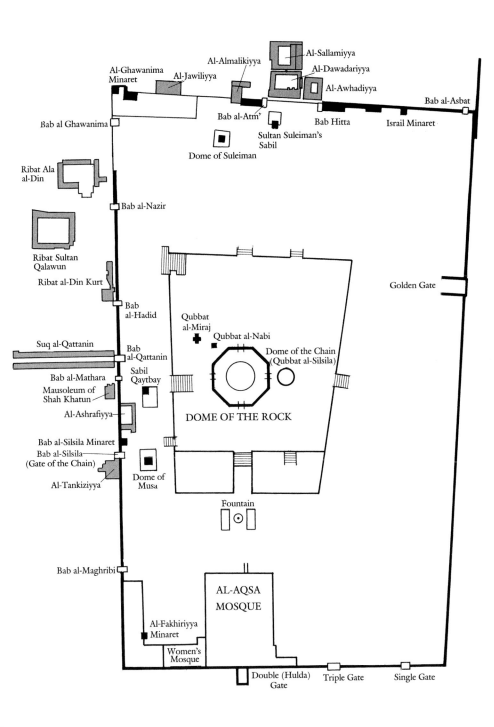

large open space and, like a magnet, drawing visitors to the city. The space on which it sits is partly empty and partly covered with olive trees and an assorted selection of structures. From the west, the Dome is not immediately striking because of the densely built city in front of it, but its gilt outline, seen from afar and embraced by the Mount of Olives to the east, still exerts a powerful attraction (Fig. 7). As one walks through the city from that direction, the Dome is invisible, but all the streets lead inescapably and almost magically to its sudden appearance at the end of the trek, behind a few scruffy walls, a selection of small stone buildings, and an unimposing set of steps. The Dome does not come into view from the north until the traveler is practically standing on the large open esplanade surrounding it.

The monument's unavoidable presence in Jerusalem has carried it into advertisements for many products. It has been a recurring image on tourist posters for Israel, for the Palestine of the Mandate period, for today's Palestine Authority, and for the Holy Land of Christian pilgrimage. It has appeared on thousands of objects— plates, textiles, ashtrays, clocks, key chains, and mementos of all sorts—found primarily in Jerusalem but available all over the Muslim and Arab world. Hardly a household or an office from Morocco to Indonesia can be found that does not exhibit some- where an image of the Dome of the Rock. Many Palestinian and Arab restaurants in the western hemisphere have its picture on menus or facades.

Most of these uses are simply instances of tourist publicity, akin to images of the Eiffel Tower or the Taj Mahal on objects of daily

7. A view from the east toward the Mount of Olives. The dome of the church of the Holy Sepulcher is in the foreground. (Israel Images / Alamy.)

use from France or India. But the ubiquity of the Dome of the Rock also derives in part from the recent fervor of Palestinian nationalism, which has anchored its expectations on a building that is indeed located in Palestine and has at times in the past been used to make a political statement, although not necessarily a national or even religious one. (For example, a French book dealing with women in the Islamic world has on its dust jacket a handsomely outlined Dome of the Rock as background to a photograph of a North African woman.) On the streets of Tehran, the Dome of the Rock is painted on exterior walls and on large advertisement panels as a pious reminder of the political struggle for the city of Jerusalem.

The form has inspired other buildings, including, in Cairo, the mausoleum of Qala'un, which juts out into a street rich in major architectural monuments. By imitating a masterpiece of early Islamic art, this late-thirteenth-century building celebrated the Muslims' recent reclamation of Palestine from the Crusaders. In Istanbul, the mausoleum of Suleyman the Magnificent, who, as we will see, was so instrumental in the creation of pre-modern Jerusalem, copied the octagonal shape of the Dome of the Rock and kept a narrow second octagon inside the building, though the external tiles gave way to an exterior colonnade. And in more recent years the grandiose and spacious mosque in front of the new airport terminal in Riyadh, Saudi Arabia, designed by an atelier from St. Louis and built by a construction firm from San Francisco, has adapted the Dome of the Rock's plan and elevation to an architectural program emphasizing communal prayer.

These and many other examples show that over the centuries the building has acquired a constant if inconsistent significance within Islamic culture. Does this power derive from its high visibility in a city full of religious memories? Does it flow from its antiquity as the earliest remaining work of Islamic art, and perhaps the earliest consciously constructed shrine of that faith? Or is it because of the building's immediately perceptible aesthetic values—its elegant massing and the brilliance of its colorful decoration? Should the Dome of the Rock be viewed as a generic architectural form, used in this particular urban context to commemorate an important moment in history, or is it a unique work of art?

To the Crusaders, this structure was the Temple of the Lord (Templum Domini)—the Jewish temple that had played such an important part in the early life and the death of Jesus. The Knights Templar, of mysterious fame in medieval cultural history, took their name from it. In the early sixteenth century, Raphael's painting of the life of the Virgin presents a beautiful image of Mary's betrothal in front of an octagonal building set on an empty platform resembling the Dome of the Rock. Around the same time, the Venetian painter Carpaccio represented St. George's triumph over a dragon in front of a fairly accurate rendition of the Dome of the Rock, for reasons that may have been both narrative and decorative. And in many northern paintings of the Crucifixion, the Dome of the Rock appears anachronistically in the background of the Cross on Golgotha, as though it symbolizes or depicts the reality of the Jerusalem on whose outskirts Jesus died.

Thus, in addition to being a beautiful urban magnet that draws visual attention to itself, the Dome of the Rock is a symbol with many connotations for Muslims, Jews, and Christians and is the main fixture of a larger holy space bathed in religious memories. Yet, curiously, the building itself is never expressly mentioned in the liturgical texts of Judaism and Christianity. Of course, many of these texts were compiled before the monument's construction. But it is strange that the Dome of the Rock does not appear in later additions to the liturgical repertoire. The holy city of Jerusalem is constantly invoked in pious and ceremonial practice and is present at all sorts of levels in these two religious traditions. Christian hymns, prayers, and services regularly allude to the city, particularly in the period from Palm Sunday to the Ascension, when the events of the Passion are recalled. And observant Jews, every day, recite the verse from Psalm 137 which commands that the holy city not be forgotten. The area of the Temple is frequently mentioned in Jewish and Christian liturgy, but never this particular building.

Islamic attitudes are less formalized than Christian and Jewish ones, largely because Islam did not develop a significant liturgical tradition nor an ecclesiastical organization to maintain a liturgy or to gather and preserve memories. Yet, within the Muslim tradition, the Haram al-Sharif is, after the Haram in Mecca and the Mosque of the Prophet in Medina, the third holiest spot on earth for the faithful. Together with the Dome of the Rock which sits on this site, it is one of only three divinely ordained mosques *(masajid Allah)*, according to Ibn Khaldun, the great theoretician of history of the late fourteenth century who echoed a commonly held belief. But not all religious thinkers shared his view. To some, like Ibn

Taymiyah, the rigorous Syrian theologian and philosopher also of the fourteenth century, the Dome of the Rock was nothing special. And in fact, the holiness of the city of Jerusalem itself was rejected by a powerful fringe of Islamic theologians and religious practitioners around this time. In short, the piety that Muslims attached to the building, the site, and the city has been far from universal or consistent in its fervor.

Variations in pious attachment to this place have occurred even in our own times. My own first visit to the Haram, in 1953, brought me to a space almost always empty and ill-kempt, whereas now it seems too small for the masses that gather there, and much care is devoted to its upkeep. The Dome of the Rock has become the main gathering place in Jerusalem for pious Muslim women to pray and listen to endless accounts of the life of the Prophet. Yet only a few decades ago it was a silent building where a few old men prayed occasionally or meditated on holy things.

Why these variations in use, if not in significance? What emotional, psychological, ideological, or other factors were involved in the creation of the Dome of the Rock, in its survival over so many centuries, and in the meanings it has acquired and shed? For it is clear even from this short introductory narrative that this is a building with a history, a building whose meaning changed over time without significant modification of its original form. This book will try to tell the building's story as it evolved in periods of calm neglect as well as conflict.

The first half of my history will focus on the fateful decades of the building's creation. In the first chapter I try to reconstruct the thoughts, ideas, and expectations associated with the (then) huge and empty area of the Haram. In Chapter 2 I describe and explain the building that arose during the last decade of the seventh century CE. Chapter 3 focuses on the changes that took place between 700 and 1100, a time when the Dome of the Rock acquired its more or less definitive Islamic identity.

Between 1100 and 1300 the whole region was engulfed in the clashes of the Crusades and in a short-lived Christianization of Jerusalem. These struggles, described in the opening section of Chapter 4, led to a new affirmation of the city's meaning in the Muslim faith and to an awareness of this particular building's significance in the wider Islamic culture. During this time the Dome of the Rock also entered the visual and emotional consciousness of the Christian world. In the peaceful centuries that followed, first under Mamluk rule from Cairo and then under Ottoman domination from Istanbul, the Dome of the Rock and the surrounding platform and esplanade acquired their modern shape, even as the building's many meanings continued to evolve.

Throughout this short book I combine what we know of the building at a particular time with what we can say about the broader historical, cultural, and aesthetic implications of the monument. And I mix this analysis of observable features and original written sources with my own hypotheses, compelled by many years of involvement with the building or by the historical logic of the space at many different times. Although I occasionally introduce scholarly arguments for individual topics, this book does not reflect in full the multiplicity of sources, discussions, and disagreements within academic communities. Scholarly documentation is, for the most part, relegated to the bibliographical essay at the end of the book, and even there I cannot vouch that I have kept up with all the work on Jerusalem that has appeared in the past decade. Some of the views developed here are the result of personal judgments and prejudices for which I offer neither excuse nor explanation.

In the final analysis, whatever meanings the building had at any one time or has now, and whatever uses it may have in the future, its most striking feature, for me, is that it is a work of art. Its sheer quality allows it to escape the constrictions of period and perhaps even of faith and culture. It was as a historian of art, as a student of the ways in which forms are created and operate to affect the senses and sensibilities of men and women, that I first approached this building over fifty years ago. Another book, starting with the religious values and history of this building, would give a very different slant to the same documents and observations upon which I draw. And indeed, the contrast between a monument of universal aesthetic value and a shrine built for and maintained by a restricted Muslim community poses a major ethical as well as political problem for our time. Can one find ways to reconcile the pious requirements and feelings of a specific community with the aesthetic values of mankind as a whole? I shall return to this question in my Conclusion.

1 THE SEVENTH CENTURY

An Empty Space Full of Memories

The date of Jerusalem's takeover by Muslim Arabs and the circumstances under which it happened are the subjects of some scholarly debate. But certainly by 640 CE, perhaps as early as 637, Muslim rule was firmly established over what was at the time a Christian holy city. It was inhabited primarily by nuns, monks, and priests and by a large service community catering to this pious establishment and to the throngs of pilgrims making their way to Jerusalem from all over the Christian world. This service community included cooks, innkeepers, carpenters, masons, engineers, stone workers, painters, and mosaicists, as well as artisans working in wood, glass, or metal. Jerusalem was a high-maintenance city where new buildings were constantly erected, old ones were ever in need of repairs, and most pious monuments were lavishly decorated. Furthermore, the city was—as it still is—a place that cultivated memories and commercialized them through souvenirs. Jews were not allowed to live in it, but they frequently came as pious visitors and kept their own memories alive.

The Space

The layout of Jerusalem affected, and was affected by, the peculiarities of the terrain on which the city was built. The walled city—more or less the same size now as it was in the second century CE—lies across the southern parts of two parallel rocky ridges (Fig. 8). The western ridge runs from Golgotha at its northern end to Mount Zion, its highest point, to the south, just outside the present city walls. The eastern hill was known over the centuries as Mount Moriah, but today it is called either the Haram al-Sharif or the Temple Mount, through the conflation of a geological formation with one of the architectural ensembles built on it. Between the two hills is a deep valley usually identified by its Greek name, Tyropoeon. Mostly filled in at its northern end, it is clearly visible to the south, near the vast open space in front of what is known today as the Western Wall—a section of the western boundary of the esplanade. Further to the northwest is a succession of relatively low ridges and gullies, but toward the southeast the terrain slopes down steeply. East of this steep slope is the deep Kidron Valley and then the Mount of Olives, which dominates the city and from which, on a good day, one can see the Mediterranean to the west and the Dead Sea to the east, with the Moabite wilderness beyond.

The seventh-century city was somewhat larger than the present Old City. Mount Zion, its highest point in the southwest corner, was included inside the walls, and a fairly extensive area at the southeast corner was enclosed by another simpler wall built on the order of the Byzantine empress Eudocia (ca. 450–460), who lived

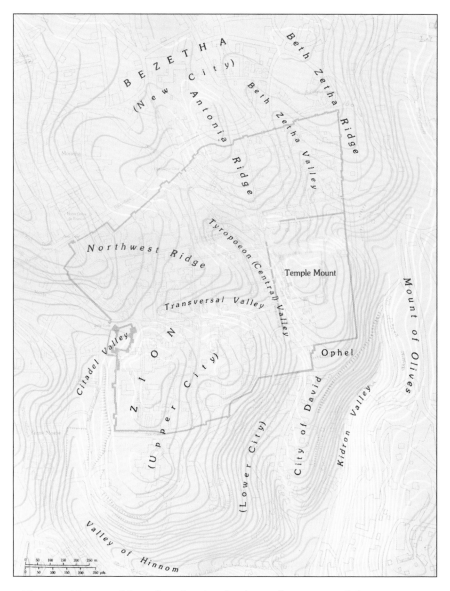

8. Topographic map of Jerusalem showing the abrupt descent toward the east and the Kidron Valley, as well as the Tyropoeon Valley between the eastern and western hills of the city. (From Bahat, *Illustrated Atlas of Jerusalem.*)

in the city for many years and was a major patron of architecture (Fig. 9). The Old City was walled for several reasons. One was symbolic: walls on the hills of Judea delineated a holy space that was different from other urban entities or from the surrounding terrain. Walls also reflected Jerusalem's origin as a Roman military camp; such cities were always enclosed and thus restricted in size and internal arrangement. Major gates on all four sides generated a grid of straight streets crossing one another, whenever possible, at right angles. The third reason for enclosure is that a simple wall served, most of the time, as sufficient defense against threats from marauding tribes of nomads who inhabited the arid lands surrounding the city. Walls also offered protection against the pilfering of sanctuaries by pilgrims.

Although we are poorly informed on the matter, the seventh-century walls were probably not as mighty and impressive as they had been earlier or would become later. The city had been sacked by the Persians in 615, and much of its defensive apparatus had been destroyed or severely damaged. For several decades, no strong leadership emerged to sponsor and implement significant programs of urban rehabilitation. The city returned from direct or indirect Persian rule to Christian hands in 628, and in 630 the Byzantine emperor Heraclius entered the city in full glory carrying the True Cross, which had been taken away by the Persians. But whatever reconstruction took place after the Christian reconquest was limited mostly to monuments of piety or to ceremonial structures, such as an elaborate gate built for the imperial procession.

Jerusalem was a city of churches. Most of them were located on

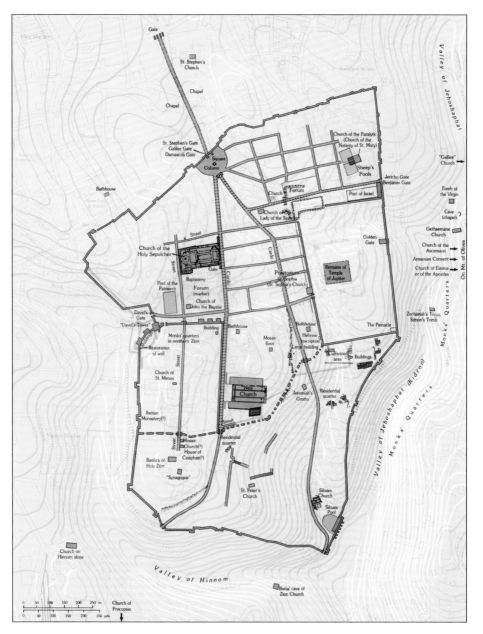

Gate

St. Stephen's
Church

Chapel

Chapel

St. Stephen's Gate
Galilee Gate
Damascus Gate

Square
Column

Bathhouse

Church of the Paralytic
(Church of the
Nativity of St. Mary)

Sheep's
Pools

Jericho Gate
Benjamin Gate

"Galilee"
Church

Tomb of
the Virgin

Cave
(chapel)

Church
(?)

Forum

Pool of Israel

Church of
Our Lady of the Spring

Street

Church of the
Holy Sepulcher

Cardo

Golden
Gate

Gethsemane
Church

Church of the
Ascension

Armenian Convent

Church of Eleona
or of the Apostles

On Mt. of Olives

Gate

Pool of the
Patriarch

Baptistery
Forum
(market)

Cardo

Praetorium
S. Sophia
(St. Sophia's Church)

Remains of
Temple
of Jupiter

David's
Gate
"David's Tower"

Church of
John the Baptist

Building

Bathhouse

Bathhouse

Zechariah's Tomb,
Simon's Tomb

Monks' Quarters

The Pinnacle

Monks' quarters
in northern Zion

Restoration
of wall

Church of
St. Menas

Street

Mosaic
floor

Hebrew
inscription
Large building

Cultivated
area

Buildings

Neo
Church

Jeremiah's
Grotto

Residential
quarter

Valley of Jehoshaphat (Kidron)

Monks' Quarters

Iberian
Monastery(?)

Street

Mosaic
Church(?)
House of
Caiaphas(?)

Residential
quarter

Street

Basilica of
Holy Zion

"Synagogue"

St. Peter's
Church

Siloam
Church

Siloam
Pool

Church on
Hinnom slope

Valley of Hinnom

Burial cave of
Zion Church

0 50 100 150 200 250 m.

0 50 100 150 200 250 yds.

Church of
Procopius

9. Jerusalem circa 640 with the major Christian sanctuaries in the western
section of the city and the extension to the south identified by what is
called Eudocia's wall. (From Bahat, *Illustrated Atlas of Jerusalem*.)

or near the western ridge of the city. The major one was the complex of the Holy Sepulcher just west of the main city street. It had been built by Constantine the Great in the first half of the fourth century and then redone by order of the Byzantine emperor Justinian in the sixth century. The complex encompassed in a single monument the Golgotha of the Crucifixion, a large congregational hall, and the tomb of Jesus, which was also of course the site of the Resurrection. An elaborate gate (fragments of which can still be seen in the shop of a pastry maker) faced eastward toward the city. It led to a large five-aisled basilica that was used primarily for collective services (Fig. 10). Behind it, an open area, later to be covered with a much larger dome, contained a *ciborium* or *tholos*—a cylindrical domed building—over Jesus' tomb. Dwellings and storage areas all around served the ecclesiastical establishment in a variety of ways.

We do not know much about the decoration of the church except through written documents, but it certainly included large mosaic panels representing appropriate scenes from the life of Christ. Little by little, much more than just the Passion came to be commemorated in this church, with which Old Testament prophets from Adam to Abraham were eventually associated. In the Christian view of the time, *there* was the *omphalos,* the navel of the universe—both a physical center marked by a specific place near Jesus' tomb and a spiritual center connecting Adam, the first sinner, to Christ, the Redeemer.

From the point of view of the Dome of the Rock to come, two features of the Holy Sepulcher complex are essential. One is the sequence congregation-commemoration-service areas, which had become standard for major Christian sanctuaries of the sixth century and which implied, placed next to one another, very different psychological and ceremonial behaviors and attitudes. The presence of this sequence differentiated large basilicas with a broad public from simple churches restricted to local congregations. The other important feature of the Holy Sepulcher complex is that it dominated the western half of the city and opened up toward the empty and ravaged space where the Second Jewish Temple and Roman pagan structures had once stood. In addition to its strictly religious associations, this monument had a socio-political agenda: to proclaim Christian victory over Judaism and paganism.

Although much diminished in visual power and much reduced in size over the centuries, the Church of the Holy Sepulcher still serves today as a focus for Christian beliefs and pious feelings (Fig. 11). This is no longer so with the second large church inside the city, the New Church of the Mother of God (the Nea), built by order of Justinian in 543 and located farther south. Excavated in the 1970s by Israeli archaeologists, this classical five-aisled basilica, with its apse set on the edge of the western ridge, dominated the Tyropoeon Valley. Like Constantine before him and the Ottoman sultan Suleyman the Magnificent much later, Justinian wanted to make his mark on Jerusalem, and his church quite consciously turned its back to the eastern half of the city, associated with Judaism, and opened toward a new Christian world to the west.

A dozen additional sanctuaries inside the walled city, and several outside, all commemorated some holy personage or event. The most interesting ones were in the Kidron Valley to the east. They included one church in the garden of Gethsemane, where Jesus prayed before his trial, and several others, nearby, dedicated to the Virgin. On the Mount of Olives an octagonal Church of the Ascension commemorated the last moments of Christ's presence on earth, an event that became conflated in the early medieval period with his return at the end of time. This conflation of events is captured in a celebrated miniature from a sixth-century Gospel book in Syriac, which copied a mosaic that existed somewhere in Jerusalem. The miniature depicts in succinct and richly symbolic form the announcement of Christ's birth (through a gesture of acceptance by the Virgin Mary and the hand of God directed toward her), the Ascension in the presence of the apostles (but not of the Virgin), and Christ's eventual return in full glory (Fig. 12). The central part of the Church of the Ascension was open to the sky, so that the faithful could see at once the spot from which Christ rose and the heavens into which he ascended. According to a report from a late seventh-century western pilgrim, lamps in the windows of the Church of the Ascension were so bright that they could be seen from the city, and light was carried down into the valley and back up into Jerusalem itself through a string of lamps that burned throughout the night.

An equally impressive, although less well documented, series of commemorative places extended southward from Jerusalem to the place of Jesus' birth in Bethlehem, barely a day's walk away. Holy places of all kinds could be found on the route between the two cities. A recently discovered octagonal church possibly dedicated to

10. Plan of the church of the Holy Sepulcher, as it has been reconstructed for the seventh century CE.

11. Exterior of the church of the Holy Sepulcher, as it appears today from the east, after major changes in the eleventh, twelfth, and nineteenth centuries. (David Sanger Photography / Alamy.)

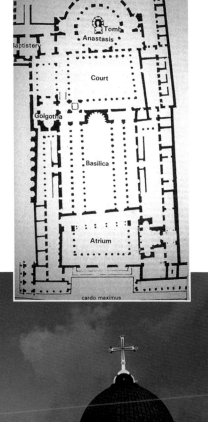

12. "The Ascension of Christ," Rabbula Gospel Book, sixth century.
(Biblioteca Nazionale, Florence, Italy; Scala / Art Resource, NY.)

the Virgin is probably just one example of the kind of sanctuaries that dotted the pilgrims' trek as they followed the traces of their holy history. The monastery of St. Sabas—though forbidding in its desert setting—was, and still is, equipped with books and scholars known all over the Christian world.

We can thus fairly easily imagine the physical shape of Christian Jerusalem around 630 CE, with its public congregational churches and more restricted sanctuaries, along with its secluded or open monastic establishments. Although relatively few of the theological debates that characterized more intellectual Christian centers like Constantinople, Antioch, or Alexandria took place in Jerusalem, pious treasures abounded there. The living quarters of several types of civilians, including a large service community, were attached to and controlled by imperial authorities under the leadership of a governor backed up by a police force and a military garrison. The Christian community may at times have been ruled by an administrator appointed by Constantinople, but in the early decades of the seventh century the patriarch of Jerusalem, one of the five acknowledged leaders of the entire Christian Church, seems to have been the dominant authority for secular as well as religious matters.

Symbols such as lights in windows and streets, the coming and going of foreign pilgrims, and formal liturgical events like processions at Easter time or other major festivals established a rhythm in the city that reflected the seasons and the liturgical calendar. This predictability was frequently punctuated, however, with earthquakes and other natural phenomena, the arrival of powerful figures from far away lands, or simply the vagaries of daily life. At a minimum, these irregularities called forth new adaptive behaviors, and sometimes they led to destruction. Quite a few accounts by visitors, often keen on providing lists of religious establishments and the number and variety of religious officials involved in the operation of a church, paint a wonderful picture of a very lively city. A late-sixth-century pilgrim from Piacenza in Italy recorded seeing in the complex of the Holy Sepulcher "armlets, bracelets, necklaces, rings, belts, emperors' crowns of gold and precious stone . . . the altar of Abraham, the Wood of the Cross . . . the sponge and reed mentioned in the Gospel . . . the onyx cup which he blessed at the Supper . . . a portrait of Blessed Mary, her girdle, and the band which she used to have on her head."

Within the organized and built-up space of piety that was Jerusalem in the early seventh century, one area was empty: the large esplanade created by Herod the Great for the Second Jewish Temple, which was demolished by the Romans in 70 CE. In the second century, a pagan temple and a large statue of the emperor Hadrian were erected there. Both were destroyed or left to collapse on their own. All of these ruins contributed blocks, paving stones, columns, capitals, and other architectural fragments to be quarried for buildings elsewhere in the city. In short, the area of the Temple was a mess; and while a late medieval description of the esplanade as being the city's dumping ground may be apocryphal, much of the debris from construction sites throughout Jerusalem may have been deposited on this vast open space. The dumping of other refuse—animal bones and the like—is less likely, given that the nu-

13. A fragment of mosaic on the floor of St. George's church in Madaba, Jordan (sixth century). The Christian buildings of the city are concentrated on the western (lower) part, and the large open space of what became the Haram al-Sharif is practically invisible. (Erich Lessing / Art Resource, NY.)

merous cisterns underneath the esplanade remained relatively free from contamination and were used for many centuries, right up until our own times.

The Madaba mosaic map, a unique visual document of the sixth century depicting the city, indicates what may be a chapel in the southeastern corner of the esplanade (Fig. 13). It would have been near the former entrance to the underground halls known as the Stables of Solomon, recently transformed into what is now called the Marwanid Mosque. Interpretation of this detail of the mosaic is still open to discussion, but it is possible, though so far not demonstrated, that a small chapel commemorating the place of the martyrdom of St. Stephen in the first century CE or the memory of James, the brother of Jesus and the first bishop of Jerusalem, stood in this location.

Two features of the esplanade that were definitely visible in the seventh century are more problematic. One is the ensemble known as the Golden Gate (Fig. 14). Its name derives from an early medieval confusion between the Greek *horeia* meaning "beautiful" (as in Acts 3:2 and 10) and the Latin *aurea* meaning "golden." The gate is located on the eastern wall of the esplanade, a relatively short distance from its northern end, and appears today as a massive block consisting of a handsome eastern facade overlooking the Kidron Valley and of two parallel aisles covered with domes on pendentives. An ongoing debate concerning the exact date of the gate has attempted to reconcile the style and techniques of construction and decoration with the complex history of Jerusalem as understood from other sources. However one is to decide between Herodian, Roman, seventh-century Christian, or seventh–eighth century Islamic dates, there can be no doubt that the rather striking remains of an originally Herodian gate existed in this location in the seventh century. It was comparable to the southern or Double Gate, which was probably also in ruins, though the Golden

14. The Golden Gate from the east, as it is today and probably has been since the thirteenth century. (Arco Images / Alamy.)

Gate appears to have been perennially closed and, for all practical purposes, useless.

The second visible feature is historically and symbolically far more important, although actually far more mysterious. The highest point of the eastern hill of Jerusalem was a large protruding rocky outcrop (roughly 18 by 13 meters), with an underground square room some 4.50 meters to the side and a neatly drilled hole

15. The Rock, seen from above. It has been cleaned and polished for centuries, and its present surface configuration is more or less the one it had in the fourteenth century. (Saïd Nuseibeh.)

of a few centimeters in diameter more or less in the middle. This Rock was originally yellowish in color like most of the limestone of Jerusalem, though today it looks much darker because of centuries of cleaning, oiling, and otherwise prepping for being seen and worshiped (Fig. 15). The underground room was initially a natural cave but had already been much altered by Late Antique times, and the neat hole was certainly man-made.

The problem is that none of the descriptions of the Jewish Temple in any of its versions—from the times of Solomon, Zerubbabel, or Herod—mention this rock, which must have been the most obvious and spectacular feature of the hill. One has to wait for the fourth century and an anonymous Christian pilgrim from Bordeaux to hear of the existence somewhere on the esplanade of a "rock with a hole" *(lapis pertusus)* anointed by Jews who came to lament the destruction of the Temple. We have no satisfactory explanation for the silence of written sources about what must have been the most prominent feature of Jerusalem's eastern ridge. Perhaps no one noticed it, or perhaps its associations were so obvious that no one felt a need to mention them. Both explanations leave much to be desired.

We have to conclude, then, that the vast and harmoniously planned Herodian Temple area, built and designed according to the orderly principles of Roman and Hellenistic architecture adjusted to the liturgical and symbolic requirements of Judaism, had, by the early seventh century, become a messy space. Its mounds of architectural fragments represented either debris dumped haphazardly from all over the city or else ruins of some earlier glorious building, now gone. A few partially visible architectural features, difficult to interpret—the several gates to the outside, the monumental walls that supported the southern part of the esplanade, and the mysterious Rock—probably stood higher than the surrounding rubble. And despite the apparent chaos, this space was bathed in memories—memories that directed the fate of the space from the seventh century onward.

Historical Memories

In order to understand the Islamic memories that would come to dominate the space and the city as a whole, we must be aware of the earlier and more elaborate (or perhaps simply better documented) Jewish and Christian memories associated with the site. These three sets of memories could be sketched independently of one another, but in reality they were all there at the same time, at once merging and separating, and contributing in this fashion to the unique flavor of the city and to the rich texture of associations that would be made with the space by medieval Muslims and perpetuated until today. For this reason, I have chosen instead to divide my discussion into three different categories—historical memories, mythical events, and eschatology—in each of which I will identify discrete Jewish, Christian, and Muslim features. In many ways all of these categories, including even the oldest Jewish memories, are examples of what may be called fluid knowledge, ill-formed but richly textured stories at a crossroads of history, literature, and piety. Thus, my three categories often merge and must be seen as somewhat artificial ways to organize information rather than clear delineations of fact, fiction, and belief.

So to begin with historical memories. We do not know today where Solomon's Temple, begun around 961 BCE, was actually located, but a great deal is known about its shape and fixtures from Biblical sources (1 Kings 5–8, 2 Chronicles 2–7, Ezekiel 40–43). It was a rectangular building set on a platform with an enclosed Holy of Holies in which the Ark of the Covenant was placed. There were two columns in front of it, a separate altar, and a large basin known as the "molten sea" presumably filled with mercury and supported by twelve sculpted oxen. The Temple's decoration of cedar and gold was certainly elaborate and probably unique for its time, but little information exists to reconstruct it in any detail.

Solomon's Temple, with whatever changes and additions may have accrued over the centuries, was pilfered and destroyed by the Assyrians in 587–586 BCE. Some fifty years later, under the leadership of Zerubbabel, a new Temple was built, probably according to the same scheme as Solomon's but without its lavish decoration and hallowed treasures like the Ark of the Covenant. This Temple underwent many alterations over the centuries, especially in the later Hellenistic period when conflicts were frequent between Greek rulers and traditional Jews attached to the Temple. Some of these changes are recorded in texts, but none are identifiable archaeologically because of the total overhaul carried out from 20 BCE onward under the patronage of Herod the Great.

The magnificent masonry of the south and southwestern borders of the Haram are from Herod's time and testify to the grandeur of his achievement. Textual references are sufficiently numerous to allow for a reasonable reconstruction of that Temple, even if the several existing attempts differ from one another in a number of details. But, except for its perimeter, some of its gates, and probably thousands of cut stones reused for centuries thereafter, nothing remains from the Temple itself, and its exact relationship to the terrain of the hill is still very much a mystery. It has also proved impossible so far to provide a reasonable function within the Temple for the large rock that is under the present dome and could not have escaped the notice of writers like Josephus, the chronicler of the destruction of the Temple in 70 CE, though he does not mention it at all.

Only hypothetically can we explain the large size and unusual location of the platform on which the Dome of the Rock is found. That platform would have covered large amounts of debris from the Herodian Temple and from the Roman one that followed it. At a time before bulldozers, it was far easier to pile remains together at a place not too far from where they fell than to move them from the site altogether. The location of the present platform may justify the hypothesis that the main part of the Temple was located directly under it or close by.

Such a long history for one of the most extraordinary holy places in the world left surprisingly few concrete traces in the memories of the seventh century. Jews alone seemed to connect the "perforated rock" with the Temple and to mourn once a year the devastation brought about by the Assyrians and the Romans. Except for Jewish sources, most medieval chronicles record fragments of this history but do not connect it specifically to any one place. Muslim rulers adopted the space as they found it but did not make a connection with the Herodian history that had created it. Crusaders and, after them, most Christian sources associated the area with Solomon as its inventor and with the lives of Christ and the Virgin as its most significant events; the building's history during the time of Herod and the uses to which the space was put after 70 CE were ignored or forgotten.

In short, the actual history of the Jewish Temple had little to do with the memories associated with the Haram. But the fact that it had been, and still was, at least to Jews, a hallowed space and the focus of yearly pilgrimages was remembered and eventually transformed into myth. And the presence of the myth of the Temple may well explain why the city of Jerusalem, initially called Iliya in Arabic (transferring into the new language its old Roman name of Ilium), became Bayt al-Maqdis, House of the Temple, a translation from Hebrew through Aramaic that recalls the Jewish sanctuary in name if not in memory. The modern Arabic name for the city, al-Quds, meaning "the Holy" (from the same root as *qadasa*, meaning "to be holy"), appeared later in the Middle Ages.

In 613 the Persian general Shahrbaraz invaded Syria, one of many episodes in the centuries-long struggle between Rome or Byzantium and whatever dynasty was ruling Iran—the Sasanians since the third century. Shahrbaraz rapidly took control of the Palestinian coastline and of Caesarea, the capital of Byzantine Palestine. Then in May 614 he besieged Jerusalem, where some local hotheads had killed a few Persian representatives. After twenty-one days of siege, Shahrbaraz entered the city, victorious. What followed was the massacre of many Christians, along with the looting of most churches and the capture of the patriarch Zachariah, who was exiled to northern Iraq, along with numerous inhabitants of the city and the relic of the True Cross from the Church of the Holy Sepulcher. Christian sources report that many Jews, who had been expelled from the city by Christian leaders in the fourth century, returned to Jerusalem after the Persian takeover and began to build or to rebuild something on the site of the Temple. But, again for unknown reasons, the Persians turned against the Jews, stopped whatever work was in progress, and once again pushed them out of Jerusalem.

Direct or indirect Christian rule was reestablished under the leadership of a local abbot, Modestus, and a number of the destroyed sanctuaries were slowly rehabilitated. In the meantime, the Byzantine emperor Heraclius moved against the Persians, and in 629, after several military victories, he negotiated the departure of Persian troops from Syria and Palestine and the return of the True Cross into Christian hands. On or around March 21, 630, a solemn ceremony, still commemorated in the liturgical calendar of the Orthodox Church, brought Heraclius back to Jerusalem. The emperor entered the city from the east, like Christ on Palm Sunday, and returned the True Cross to the Holy Sepulcher.

Many scholars believe that this ceremonial and highly symbolic event was marked by the construction of a monument. Noting that the Golden Gate has been occasionally dated to the time of Methodius (who died in 630), they have imagined it as the triumphal arch for the return of the True Cross. Some scholars have even argued that the original Herodian Temple area was square, not rectangular, and that its northern boundary, originally slightly to the north of the platform of the Dome of the Rock, was extended to its present location in order to accommodate the ceremonial requirements of this event. We shall probably never know whether this hypothesis corresponds to the truth, and in such instances of insufficient evidence it is wiser to stick to the traditional account, which has Heraclius entering Jerusalem through the city gate known today as St. Stephen's gate, to the immediate north of the esplanade.

The event itself certainly was a major episode in the religious and political history of the city, whether or not it left architectural traces. All the more curious, then, that the occasion was so sporadically recalled by later Christian sources other than the Orthodox liturgy. The reason may be simply that, for mysterious reasons, Heraclius removed the Cross to Constantinople just five years later, in 635, right before the arrival of Muslim Arab forces in Jerusalem. Heraclius' victory and the return of the Cross thus became irrelevant to later times in Jerusalem. These events were spectacularly depicted in Piero della Francesca's fifteenth-century frescoes in Arezzo, but such depictions are rare within the rich pictorial repertoire of medieval Christianity, and the story itself was all but forgotten.

After 634 and the departure of Heraclius, the Byzantine military presence in Jerusalem probably weakened, and the countryside around Jerusalem became infested with bandits and roaming nomadic tribesmen. Authority in the city was in the hands of the patriarch Sophronius, an ecclesiastical figure. He was a learned and pious man, as well versed in classical Greek culture as he was in theology. In one of his letters Sophronius complained that he was not able to go to Bethlehem for Christmas because of dangers on the short road between the two cities. In a sermon a few days later, he related that the offending Arab tribesmen "boast that they will conquer the world." These words have been interpreted to mean that the tribesmen involved were Muslim. While such an interpretation cannot be entirely excluded, this explanation implies a doctrinal sophistication on the part of the marauders that is hardly plausible less than two decades after the formation of an Islamic polity in Medina, far away in west central Arabia. These troublemakers were more likely traditional highway robbers rather than carriers of a new sectarian message.

The real thrust of the Muslim attack on Byzantine forces in Syria and Palestine took place elsewhere: along the Mediterranean coast, where the Christian capital of Palestine, Caesarea, and the main trade routes to and from Egypt were located, and on the western edges of the semi-desertic Arabian steppe toward Damascus. Jerusalem was not a target of major significance, and most likely Sophronius surrendered the city to a secondary tribal leader converted to Islam, Khalid ibn Thabit al-Fahmi. A formal treaty that would guarantee the safety of Christian places of worship, as later sources imply, may or may not have been signed by Christian and Muslim authorities. But with or without such a treaty, these spaces remained in Christian hands for several centuries. In practice, what the agreement meant was that most of the buildings and properties in the northern and especially western parts of the city could not be used, destroyed, or otherwise transformed by Muslims. Recently arrived Arab immigrants and Jews who were again allowed to live in the city settled in the eastern section, to the north and south of the Temple platform. The details of these settlements are not known, but the basic scheme is reasonable enough.

There is, however, another narrative of the events leading to the

Muslim takeover of Jerusalem. This is primarily a Muslim narrative, but some of its features are found in Christian sources as well. According to this version of the story, the patriarch Sophronius wished to negotiate only with the Muslim commander of the faithful, the caliph 'Umar, who allegedly was with Muslim forces moving toward Damascus and central Syria. The caliph agreed to come to Jerusalem, and when he arrived nearby, he was dressed in simple and unprepossessing clothes. He was met by Sophronius, himself outfitted in the full regalia of his ecclesiastical office within the Church. Sophronius took 'Umar on a tour of Jerusalem, showing him first the Holy Sepulcher and inviting him to pray there. 'Umar refused, on the grounds that his action might be construed later as an assertion of Muslim claim to the place of the caliph's prayer (as happened much later, when the small Mosque of 'Umar was built facing the entrance to the Holy Sepulcher).

Then the patriarch led the caliph to the area of the Temple where, under a mass of refuse, 'Umar discovered the Rock and recognized it as a place mentioned by the Prophet, but without specifying why and in what circumstances the Prophet had seen it. The two dignitaries began then to clear the Rock together. As the time of prayer approached, Ka'b al-Ahbar, a Jewish convert to Islam who was a major religious and intellectual figure in Palestine, proposed that prayer be held north of the Rock, thus putting a place vaguely connected with the Jewish Temple between the praying caliph and Mecca. 'Umar pointed out the ambiguity of the proposed place for prayer and set himself south of the Rock to pray.

This version has been embellished over centuries of telling and retelling and reflects the hagiography that, in some circles at least, surrounded the person of the caliph ʿUmar: he led an ascetic and simple life, he owned only one robe whose washing delayed by a day his arrival in Jerusalem, he behaved like an equal with all his companions, and he ate sparingly. The contrast is total, at least in Muslim sources, with the Christian patriarch in his beautiful liturgical vestments and surrounded by a colorful clergy and acolytes of all sorts.

We have no way to know which version of the takeover is closer to the truth. But in whatever manner it happened, the entry of Muslims into Jerusalem was a peaceful and relatively low-key event—a curious paradox if one considers that Christians had just recently broadcast the city's holiness far and wide at the time that the True Cross was returned to it, and if one recalls the military strength and prestige of the Byzantine Empire. Something had sapped the collective will of Christians in Palestine and the Levant as a whole. Perhaps the explanation is that Christians did not see Islam as a threat to their existence, and Muslim Arabs, for their part, were more impressed by the culture they encountered than bent on its eradication. Much of what happened in Jerusalem during the centuries to come, more or less until the arrival of the Crusaders in 1099, can best be explained as an outgrowth of the relatively peaceful climate established in the city in the 630s.

Most likely, a mosque was built on the ruins of the Temple Mount—possibly the mosque described by a western pilgrim around 690 as an "oblong house of prayer, which they [the Muslims, called Saracens in the text] pieced together with uprights planks and large beams over some ruined remains." Up to three thousand people could fit there, according to this western observer. The implication of this text is that only minimal clearing preceded the construction of what seems to have been a makeshift building. But the procedure of erecting or outlining a space for the gathering of Muslims is typical of early Islamic settlements, in which a place was needed for Muslims to pray as well as to handle common political, social, and cultural concerns.

The decades following the takeover of Jerusalem witnessed the settlement in the city of Jews and especially of Muslim Arabs. The names of some of the latter have been preserved, and many contemporary residents of Jerusalem claim descent from these early settlers. In ways that cannot be reconstructed for lack of evidence, the area of the Herodian Temple was slowly cleared of debris, the platform on which the Dome of the Rock stands was formed, and some of the vaults and gates in the southern section of the esplanade were repaired and restored. Jewish labor seems to have been involved in some of this work. So also was Christian labor, and the story has come down to us of a local archdeacon who went to work on the platform to improve his income. He was asked by the patriarch himself to stop working for the "atheists" and was even promised employment and an increase in salary. The archdeacon agreed to leave his work for the Muslim authority, but two days later he was back on the Haram, where he was stricken by divine wrath for refusing, in spite of many entreaties from his coreligionists, to leave a job that was seen as antagonistic to Christianity.

However the work got done, the important point is that these were the decades during which the boundaries of a restricted Muslim space were defined and made to coincide with the shape of Herod's Temple. How historically conscious this definition was is hard to know. Did the Muslims simply preserve a space from which they, little by little, consciously or not, appropriated many components of the religious memories associated with it? Or did they feel they were restoring, in a new version and with new associations and practices, the Temple that God had originally ordered Solomon to build? We have no certain answer to these questions today, and probably there was none in the seventh century, for different people and different social classes within each ethnic or religious group answered the question in their own way, reflecting their individual beliefs, passions, and historical understanding.

The caliph Mu'awiyah, founder of the Umayyad dynasty that would dominate the Islamic world until 750, ruled Jerusalem from 661 to 680. A late convert to Islam who joined a winning side rather than acting from deeply felt belief, Mu'awiyah was an imaginative and forceful politician who successfully managed the numerous factions of the early Islamic community and the competing tribes from Arabia. In 658 he met in Jerusalem with 'Amr ibn al-'As, the conqueror of Egypt, in order to resolve the conflict that opposed Mu'awiyah to 'Ali, the son-in-law of the Prophet. They failed to resolve their disagreements satisfactorily, but according to the chronicler al-Tabari, who wrote over two centuries later, Amr ibn al-'As greeted Mu'awiyah as the "prince of the Holy Land" *(amir ard al-muqaddas),* a title suggesting Mu'awiyah's unique association with the region.

Where they met is unknown, but it is reasonable to imagine that the vast esplanade, which had become the center of the Muslim presence in Jerusalem, would have served as the proper venue for a political gathering of such major importance to the Muslim community. In 660, after he was chosen as caliph, homage was paid to Mu'awiyah in Jerusalem, where he received a crown. The Christian source who reported the coronation mentions that Mu'awiyah prayed at Golgotha (presumably inside the Holy Sepulcher), in Gethsemane, and at the tomb of Mary, also located in the Kidron Valley. No Muslim source mentions this event, and its actual occurrence is in doubt. But the Christian text probably reflected something else about these early decades of Umayyad rule—that Jerusalem had become a significant place to Muslims and that this significance involved power and politics as well as piety. The point is reflected in a later proclamation that Mu'awiyah and his son were "kings" of the Holy Land.

The vast esplanade on Mount Moriah was probably permanently under construction. Some scholars have attributed Jerusalem's first mosque to this period and have argued that Mu'awiyah initiated the architectural planning that led eventually to the building of the Dome of the Rock. The important point for us here is that the Muslim holy space in Jerusalem had a secular dimension. But we must not forget that the separation between secular and religious values or even ceremonies was at that time far less precise than it would become in the nineteenth and twentieth centuries.

Before turning from historical memories to mythological events, an important word must be said about the *qiblah*, the Muslim direction for prayer. Although the Qur'an does not explicitly say so, the original direction for prayer was Jerusalem. The Prophet Muhammad followed Jewish and Judeo-Christian practices until 624, when, in the second year of the *hijrah* (literally, "migration," the year, 622 CE, when the Prophet moved from Mecca to Medina and the first year of the Muslim calendar), he turned away from them and proclaimed the sacred Mosque of Mecca, the Masjid al-Haram, as the proper direction for prayer. This point is made several times in the second *surah* (chapter) of the Qur'an, especially in verses 112 and following, without referring to Jerusalem by name: God "has turned man from the *qiblah* to which he was accustomed toward a *qiblah* that shall please men, turning their faces in the direction of the Meccan sanctuary." This new direction became a central feature of Muslim doctrine and piety, and the old one is mentioned only in commentaries on the Qur'an as the direction of prayer observed by the People of the Book, that is, Jews and Christians.

The change in the *qiblah* established a universal axis of Muslim religious practice that would become an essential component of esoteric mysticism as well as mundane daily prayers. In early Islamic liturgical thought and behavior, Jerusalem played no real role; it was viewed as merely a brief stopover in the formation of Muslim religious life. But in daily reality, Jerusalem's role in the observance of Islam may well have been more complex. In a mosque built in the late seventh century in Wasit (Iraq) by al-Hajjaj, one of the most powerful and creative governors of early Islamic times and a devoted defender of Umayyad imperial ambitions, the *mihrab*—the niche indicating, among other things, the direction for prayer—is oriented toward Jerusalem rather than Mecca. The anomaly was soon corrected, and it could have been a mistake, as mistakes did occasionally occur in the calculation of the correct *qiblah*. But it could also have been purposeful, reflecting a lingering ideology from an earlier practice, or perhaps the uncertainties of a raging civil war between the Umayyad caliphs and Meccan political leaders.

In a deeper sense and with ramifications to which we shall return, alone among the great sanctuaries of Islam, Jerusalem developed an area called the Haram, just as Mecca did. In Mecca, *Haram* is used as an adjective ("sacred") modifying the common word for mosque *(masjid);* but in Jerusalem *Haram* itself is a noun ("sanctuary"), eventually modified by the adjective *sharif* ("noble"). These are, of course, much later phenomena, but they may well have reflected memories of the few years when Jerusalem was indeed *the* Haram, that is, the principal magnet for all Muslims.

Mythical Events

Many of the more or less accurate and appropriate historical associations made with the vast esplanade of the Temple were enriched and even transformed by mythical components. Some of these were fictive embellishments on historical facts; others were legends that could not possibly have involved Jerusalem. The sources for these myths, almost all written later than the time they describe and almost always reflecting popular oral traditions, are usually impossible to date accurately, but we know that many of them appeared fairly soon after the Muslim conquest. With these myths and legends we enter into a hazy zone of evidence more true to the general atmosphere they evoke and the influence they exerted than to any specific events of history.

Such is the case, for instance, with the story of Abraham, whose sacrifice of Isaac was connected with the Rock of Jerusalem by Jews and, at times, Christians, more rarely by Muslims, for whom Abraham was clearly associated with Mecca and the construction of the Ka'bah as the house of God. The reason for the association of Jerusalem with Abraham seems to have been either an accidental confusion between, or a deliberate conflation of, the "land of Moriah" to which Abraham takes his son and "Mount Moriah," the name of the eastern ridge of Jerusalem. In Mecca and in the Holy Sepulcher, the commemoration of Adam eventually joined that of Abraham, with several other prophets or heroes of sacred history following suit: Jacob with his pillow of stone and his ladder and several Zachariahs from the Old and New testaments. Even Moses makes an appearance, although canonical history explicitly says that he never reached Palestine, the Promised Land. At some point, Muslims began to associate Jesus' birth with a place in the southeastern corner of the esplanade, although the appearance there of "the Cradle of Jesus," which was until recently shown to pilgrims and tourists, may well have occurred considerably later than the seventh century.

Two mythical associations that derive from historically demonstrable events have played a particularly important role in memories of Jerusalem. One is the symbolically powerful presence of Solomon's palace next to his Temple. Medieval traditions in all three religions gave far more importance to this structure than to the Temple itself. The Biblical text and even more so Jewish legends, as well as later Muslim ones, depict Solomon's palace as a grandiose masterpiece built, among other reasons, to greet the Queen of Sheba. The latter was the ruler of far away Yemen, whose intellectual brilliance was successfully challenged by Solomon. According to a striking Qur'anic passage (27:44) that underwent many later developments, he fooled her by creating a pool or pavilion of crystal so transparent that it looked like water. To cross it, she lifted her skirts and showed her legs, which were those of an animal.

This story, so frequently illustrated in medieval sculpture and painting, has many implications for understanding the visual culture of the Middle Ages, as well as for the social and cultural history of Jerusalem. We have no clear indication of where Solomon's palace was located; but according to Jewish legend, his throne was next to the Temple, thus presumably in the area of the esplanade. The throne itself was covered with gold and studded with precious stones; gold sculptures of animals adorned its steps, while on the top a symbolic dove attacked an eagle. A candlestick with fourteen branches containing images of patriarchs, pious men, and prophets was set above the throne, and the area around it included places for religious and secular dignitaries to join Solomon in majesty. The throne of Solomon was later transformed into the throne of the Persian king Khosro and eventually became a standard feature of medieval princely iconography. The importance of the story for our purposes is that, even though Solomon's palace and throne were connected to a religious place, the details illustrate again the profoundly secular vein in the memories associated with the Haram in the seventh century.

Another legendary transformation of an actual historical event, or at least a historically plausible one, concerns the arrival of the caliph 'Umar in Jerusalem. Various medieval writers attempted to fit the story into the setting of the city. Thus the caliph and his companions (Muslim texts rarely, if ever, mention them as an army) camped at the southern end of the Kidron Valley while the last negotiations with the patriarch Sophronius were taking place. One of the companions fell into a well, which turned out to be an entrance to Paradise, and he came back with a branch from the Lotus Tree *(sidra al-mantaha),* which, according to the Qur'an (53:146), was found at the edge between the earth and the kingdom to come. Other traditions, already known to Jews, located the entrance to Hell in the Kidron Valley—or, in a more general way, the space of eternal life.

I shall return to this eschatological theme in the next section, and to its connection with another legend associated specifically with the Rock. According to an early Muslim tradition, the Rock was the place from which God ascended into heaven after having completed the creation of the universe. Certain indentations on the Rock were interpreted as the imprints of God's feet. The story was eventually rejected by Muslim religious orthodoxy as being impious in implying the corporeality of God, which contradicted basic Muslim theology. But in the late seventh century, this interpretation of God's footprints was still accepted and may have influenced the building of the Dome of the Rock.

And finally, on a more mundane level, the Prophet Muhammad, who had visited Jerusalem during a visionary trip (a story to which we shall also return), was asked by skeptical Meccans to describe the city. He had not seen much of it because he was traveling by night. So the archangel Gabriel uprooted the city and set it in front of him in Mecca, without his audience being aware of it, thus making is possible for Muhammad to describe Jerusalem accurately. In the fourteenth century this story, mixing a plausible event (a visit by the Prophet to Jerusalem) with miraculous myth (the uprooting of the city), was illustrated in a Persian manuscript whose fragments have remained in an album kept in Istanbul (Fig. 16). The city of Jerusalem carried by the archangel is striking for having practically no resemblance to anything known about the actual Jerusalem. The city itself had already become a myth that could be depicted in any way pleasing to a painter or a patron.

Eschatology

The story of 'Umar's companion literally falling into Paradise and miraculously returning, as well as the connection of the Rock with the presence of God on earth, leads to the last category of associations made with the Haram before any significant building was erected on it in the seventh century. This category is eschatology, which deals with the end of time and the beginning of eternal life. Each of the three monotheistic faiths developed a vision of this

event. For Judaism, it involved the coming of the Messiah. In Christianity and Islam, it became tied to a divine Judgment that would separate the elect, who would enter Paradise, from the eternally (or, in Islam, temporarily) damned.

The seventh century witnessed a revival of messianic texts among Jews and Christians that mixed contemporary events like the taking of Jerusalem by the Muslims with the establishment of an empire of evil before eternal salvation. One Jewish source identifies two emperors, the first associated with Byzantium, the other with Islam. And the latter is the one who will rescue the Jews and create a new kingdom in Jerusalem. According to another source, a king of Ishmael (the generic term for the descendants of Abraham through Hagar, identified as Arabs), presumably an Umayyad ruler, restores the Temple by flattening the surface of Mount Moriah and building a mosque on top of the Rock. In other Jewish sources, which had an impact on the Christian book of Revelation, a burnished Jerusalem of gold and precious stones will descend over the existing city and shine down on the world.

The Christian vision is more complex in that it involves the whole known world, but it too ends in Jerusalem, where the Resurrection of all men and women will begin and the Judgment will take place as Christ returns to earth surrounded by the celestial

16. Detail from "The Prophet Muhammad being shown Jerusalem carried by angels," fourteenth century. Note the totally fictional character of the city crossed by rivers. (From *Mi'raj-Nameh [Book of the Ascension]*, Istanbul, Top Kapi Seray 2154, fol. 107a.)

host. And for Muslims, the angel of death, Isra'fil, will stand on the Rock and sound the end of time with his trumpet. The Ka'bah will be uprooted in Mecca and transported to the Haram. A bridge, identified with the "straight path" *(sirat al-mustaqim)* of the first *surah* of the Qur'an, will span the Kidron Valley so that the elect can cross over to the Mount of Olives and reach Paradise after being judged on the Haram. Later Muslim imagination identified quite precisely the functions of various spots on the Haram in the procedures of this ultimate trial. One of the most touching images to emerge from Muslim thought about the events of the Judgment is found in a work by the great theologian al-Ghazali. It depicts resurrected men and women, some dressed and others naked, being carried toward God by a host of different wild and domesticated animals.

Whatever specifics of decorative rhetoric were introduced over the centuries by Jews, Christians, or Muslims, Jerusalem in the seventh century was the site prepared and groomed to hail the end of time and to proclaim a reward for the just and punishment for the wicked. Regardless of the idiosyncrasies of each religion, all of them looked forward to the moment when, within the walled city and its eastern extension, directly or through signs, God would return to earth and release the children of Adam from original sin, bringing peace, justice, and happiness to those who were found to be deserving. That spirit of expectation was part of the city's inheritance. It could and still can be found wherever there are Jews, Christians, and Muslims. Because this hope was focused on a time to come and events that had not yet happened, it lent itself to end-less growth and to unusual manifestations, even in our own time.

So, to summarize. By the end of the seventh century, the Haram had been cleared as a vast and more or less flat space. Its outer walls to the east and probably to the south and southwest were still in disrepair, but its main entrances were functioning. A sim-ple mosque had been constructed somewhere, probably in the southern part of the esplanade. The space of the Haram was rather empty and unprepossessing in a city still reeling from the destruc-tions carried out by the Persians in 615. But this space was al-ready full of stories, legends, and expectations. The long and com-plicated history of its monuments was associated with powerful figures—David, Solomon, Herod, Jesus, Mu'awiyah—and major events, such as construction of the Temple, destruction by the Assyrians and Romans, invasion by the Persians, and the Muslim takeover. These major men and events, as well as many secondary ones associated with the Haram, were connected to one another through an ever-changing political, religious, and mythical web.

Even straightforward events like the Persian and Muslim con-quests acquired so many layers of legend that we no longer know the truth. Nor does it matter, for this space was a refuge for a mas-sive accumulation of facts and myths. By trying to separate them from one another, contemporary historians often betray their own calling as seekers after truth. For the truth of this moment, in the seventh century, was a medley. And to this medley of known fea-tures one has to add the extraordinary component of a world to come, not simply the end of the norms by which mankind lives but also the divine judgment passed on all men and women throughout the ages and everywhere.

In short, the Haram, like the whole city of Jerusalem, has to be imagined as a damaged physical space bathed in a mythified history and swaddled in a grandiose hope. Without an awareness of the peculiar character of the city at that time, the significance of what happened to it around 690 CE cannot be understood.

2

700

A New Building, Its Sources, Meanings, Impact

The octagonal arcade inside the Dome of the Rock contains, above the main part of the mosaic decoration and on both sides of the arcade, a mosaic inscription some 240 meters long. It ends on its outer face, roughly in the southeastern corner, with the following statement: "Has built this dome the servant of God, the Imam al-Ma'mun, Commander of the Faithful, in the year 72 [691–692 CE]. May God accept it and be pleased with him. Amen, Lord of the worlds, praise to God." The ruler named in the inscription, al-Ma'mun, was, in fact, caliph in Baghdad between 813 and 833, at least 122 years later than the date provided by the monument. The name of the original sponsor of the building, the Umayyad caliph 'Abd al-Malik, was excised and replaced with that of a successor from a different dynasty. But whoever made the change did not go so far as to modify the date. It is as though the glory or the benefits attached to the construction of the building could be transmitted to a succession of rulers, but the time of the construction was fixed once and forevermore. Yet what appears at first to be an almost

17. Mosaic detail in southeastern section of the octagonal arcade, with the date corresponding to 691 CE and the name of al-Ma'mun. (Saïd Nuseibeh.)

childish mistake may well have profound implications for the significance of the building (Fig. 17).

As early as 1862, the French traveler and scholar Melchior de Vogüé knew about this change in the caliph's name. And scholars up to our own time have puzzled over the meaning of the date. Does it, as is usually the case, indicate the time of the monument's completion, or rather does it represent the time of its inception? Does it record the inauguration of the building, or alternatively could it signify the date of the initial "ground-breaking"? These questions may seem a tad pedantic, since we are speaking of a gap of only a few years at best. Most of the building did not involve complex technology in construction, and the project probably moved along quickly once its basic design was complete. Only the interior decoration, where the date of the building actually appears, may have required some time to complete.

Yet the question of timing is not unimportant when one tries to fit the date of the inscription with what we know of Jerusalem's history in this period. The six years that elapsed between 'Abd al-Malik's assumption of power in 685 and the date of the inscription (691) were fraught with almost continuous political and military struggle within the Muslim commonwealth. Mecca, the spiritual hub of the new faith, had been taken over by a local leader, Ibn al-Zubayr, who was trying to resuscitate an older form of Muslim piety associated with local Arabian practices. He even managed to rebuild the Ka'bah, the holiest sanctuary of the new faith. Ibn al-Zubayr's brother started an uprising in Iraq in support of this movement, and one of the caliph's own relatives initiated a revolt against him in Damascus. Rumblings could even be heard on the Anatolian frontier with Byzantium, and Byzantine agents were active among the Christian settlements of the Lebanese mountains.

'Abd al-Malik defeated Ibn al-Zubayr's brother in Iraq and between 690 and 692 returned triumphant to his capital in Damascus. Meanwhile, the brilliant Umayyad general al-Hajjaj reestablished Umayyad power in Mecca and had the Ka'bah rebuilt as it had been at the time of the Prophet. Disorders among Christians were smoothed, and the frontier with Byzantium became relatively quiet once again. As internal power and coherent rule were established, 'Abd al-Malik initiated several major changes in the administrative structure and symbolic appearance of the empire. Arabic replaced Greek, Aramaic, and Pahlevi as the official administrative language for communications from North Africa to Central Asia. By 698–699 gold and silver coinage without images but with written proclamations became standard and would remain so in most Muslim lands into the twenty-first century.

The construction of the Dome of the Rock can easily be seen as one of the accomplishments of this striking decade during which the Umayayd dynasty reestablished its dominion, and the date of 691 could be interpreted as the beginning of the construction of the building. On the other hand, if we take into account the various events that had transpired amidst the ruins of the Herodian Temple, the memories associated with the area, and the presence in Jerusalem of a permanent work force competent in building and decorating techniques, we can equally well imagine a slow process of construction that could have begun as early as the 660s, during the reign of the caliph Mu'awiyah, and reached completion by 691.

We shall probably never be able to resolve this question, since later written sources rarely reflect such mundane details of architectural construction. The few original documents we possess about building practices in the city—papyri from Egypt recording the departure of workers to Jerusalem and the attribution of tax funds for the city—deal mostly with the first decade of the eighth century and involve construction of the Aqsa Mosque and possibly of administrative and living quarters to the south of the Haram. As we shall see when we look at the building's architecture in more detail, the visual and technological logic of the Dome of the Rock supports the impression of a single, strongly felt idea and purpose for the building, and it favors the hypothesis that the project was begun in 691 and completed fairly rapidly. But other features, like the construction of the platform on which the building is located, required time, effort, and a vision, if not indeed a master plan, for the Haram as a whole. And those requirements would favor an earlier date for the building's conception.

The actual construction of the Dome of the Rock was supervised by two men, Rajah ibn Haywah and Yazid ibn Salam, who, according to the sources that have come down to us, controlled the funds made available by 'Abd al-Malik in Damascus. Little is known about Yazid ibn Salam. He was from a local family and born in Jerusalem; his role may have been as liaison with the immediate community. Rajah ibn Haywah, by contrast, was a scholar and political adviser as well as a frequent emissary for 'Abd al-Malik. Having been involved with the politics and administration of Palestine, he was a recognized authority on its holy places. The presence of this sort of double expertise—one supervisor attuned to local needs and possibilities, the other connected to a remote caliphate and the theological dimensions of the faith—illustrates a constant leitmotiv in explanations of the Dome of the Rock: the equilibrium, or tension, it exhibits between local and pan-Islamic traditions and practices.

However its construction came about, we can approach a consideration of the building itself in two ways. The first describes its physical appearance and its visual impact within the city. This description of the building includes the elements and composition that form its architectural skeleton and musculature, and of course the brilliant decoration that makes up its skin. Once these features are properly defined, we will be able to turn to the more exciting, and sometimes speculative, project of interpreting the building— of attempting to explain what it meant to the people who built it in the last decade of the seventh century, and how it was used at the time of its creation.

Architecture

The Dome of the Rock is an annular or ringlike building consisting of a dome, initially built in wood, 20.44 meters in diameter, set on a high drum containing sixteen windows and resting on a circle made up of four piers and twelve columns, with three columns between each pair of piers. This cylindrical core is set over the Rock and is surrounded by a double octagon (Fig. 18). The exterior octagon consists of eight wall faces, each 20.59 meters in length and 9.50 meters in height. The walls are built of stone and exhibit on the outside seven shallow bays, the five central ones each incorporating a window made of a simple and repeated plaster grid. A parapet 2.60 meters in height and only 0.90 meters in width is set over the wall and consists of thirteen arched openings originally decorated with glass mosaics (Fig. 19).

In each of the four cardinal directions are doors 2.55 meters

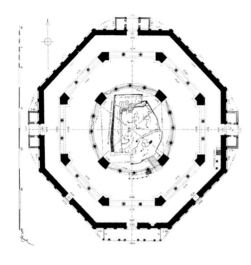

18. Plan of the Dome of the Rock. (K. A. C. Creswell; Ashmolean Museum, Oxford.)

19. Section of the Dome of the Rock. (K. A. C. Creswell; Ashmolean Museum, Oxford).

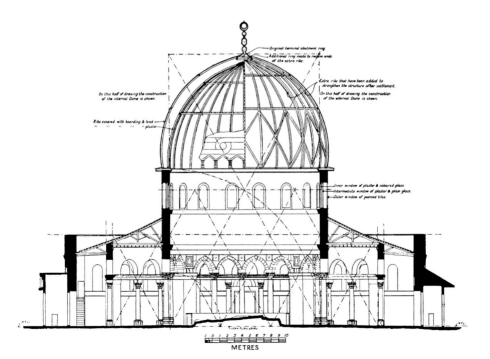

METRES

wide and 4.35 meters high. The doorways, with their two massive stone lintels, are covered on their lower faces with original bronze plaques. All doorways but the southern one are preceded by a portico with a brick barrel vault resting on four columns; the southern one has eight columns. Their present shape is ascertained from the early tenth century, but no distinctions seem to have been made originally among the four doorways, which were still standing in the fourteenth century, as we know from a representation of the Dome of the Rock sculpted in the decoration of a mosque built in Cairo during that period (Fig. 20). The entrances we see today were reconstructed in the second half of the twentieth century (Fig. 21).

Between the outer wall and the central circular arcade stands an octagonal arcade of eight piers and sixteen columns. The piers are of stone masonry, and the columns vary in height and in the order of their capitals; some are Corinthian, others are composite. Their bases also vary in size and height, indicating that the columns were rescued from the remains of one or more Herodian, Classical, or Christian buildings and reused. Above the columns, wooden tie-beams cross beneath the arches, providing flexibility and resilience to a building that would have to withstand earthquakes (Fig. 22). The width of these tie-beams, corresponding to the width of the masonry of the arches, allowed them to be used as walkways for the repair of walls and decoration. But most importantly, these beams were covered with sheets of bronze or brass decorated with floral designs. Sixteen patterns are found on these sheets: fifteen occur only once, and one is repeated nine times. We have no satis-

20. Representation of the
Dome of the Rock on the Sul-
tan Hasan madrasah, Cairo,
mid-fourteenth century.
(K. A. C. Creswell; Ashmolean
Museum, Oxford)

factory explanation for the current location of the repeated designs; this could have resulted simply from careless repairs or restorations.

The obvious effect of the beams and their decoration is to provide the octagon with a lintel-like horizontal surround that creates
honorific passageways to the Rock itself. But close examination of
the patterns of decoration elicits something rather curious. Al-

21. Portico and doorway, as reconstructed, probably accurately, in the twentieth century.

22. Segment of the octagonal arcade, showing the tie-beams and marble covering of the outer wall. (Saïd Nuseibeh.)

though designed according to the same basic principle—long bands of vine-based motifs framed by a garland of leaves—there are clear differences among these continuous and repetitive patterns, and they forecast the later arabesques of Islamic art, with their patterns organized around a central pivot (a vase or a tree) that divides the motif into two sections (Fig. 23). The simplest interpretation of these variations is an aesthetic one: they served to enrich architectural surfaces with contrasts of color and light modulated by vegetal patterns. But the possibility of more precise iconographic meanings should not be excluded.

The two ambulatories now have different ceilings from the original ones. The original ceiling of the outer ambulatory can be imagined as consisting simply of rafters that were carved and painted; at a later period, inscriptions have been preserved with dates of restoration. The ceiling we see today consists of large plaques of molded plaster set on a bed of leather. As for the inner ambulatory, nothing from the original ceiling remains, and what we see now is a series of eighteenth-century wooden coffers, many of which once had ceramic inlays. That something similar to these coffers existed in the twelfth century is known from texts. It is possible, although archaeologically by no means certain, that a source of natural light existed in the upper part of the inner ambulatory—a zone of the building that today is in total darkness.

The columns of the circular arcade that surrounds the Rock were, like those of the octagonal arcade, reused from older buildings. The arches, 1.66 meters in width and of the same dimension as the drum they support, are now slightly pointed, but this ap-

23. Decorated seventh-century bronze plaques on tie-beams.
(K. A. C. Creswell; Ashmolean Museum, Oxford)

pearance is the result of their being reset in marble in the sixteenth century. Earlier arches, if covered with mosaics, were probably semicircular. The drum of the dome is built of stone and pierced by sixteen windows, also with semicircular arches. The structure of the dome was described by a tenth-century geographer and traveler from Jerusalem: "The dome comprises three layers: the first is composed of wooden planks decorated with paintings; the second is composed of bars of iron interlaced so as to resist the pressure of the wind; and the third one is made of wood covered with sheets [of lead or brass]." This double structure of wood with intermediary iron braces is (minus the covering of brass) the shape of the dome as it existed in the early part of the twentieth century (Fig. 24). It is is therefore reasonable to conclude that the major restoration of 1027–1028, probably coming after an earthquake (to which I shall return in Chapter 3), restored the dome to the shape it had at the beginning in the late seventh century.

The dome erected in 1999 is covered with an aluminum alloy that produces a gilded effect, and it imitates the one built in 1960–1962. It stands in sharp contrast with the dull lead-covered dome that existed before 1960. The earliest written sources mention the golden appearance of the cupola, and the Umayyad structure probably displayed this gilded effect from the beginning, although how it was achieved is unknown. A finial on top of the dome is mentioned by the local geographer al-Muqaddasi, but unfortunately he does not describe it. It may have consisted of several metal balls set on a spike. A crescent, like the one that tops the dome now, was unlikely in the early Umayyad period but not impossible, since crescents are known to have existed in the sanctuary of Mecca and are represented a few times in the interior mosaic decoration of the Dome of the Rock.

At first glance, the architecture of the Dome of the Rock is one of utter simplicity whose character and principal features can be perceived immediately from both outside and inside. A thin wall,

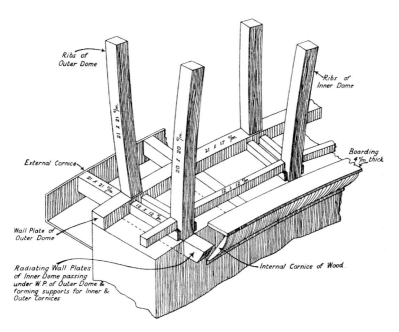

24. Construction of original dome. (K. A. C. Creswell;
Ashmolean Museum, Oxford)

minimally articulated on the exterior with similar doors on the
four cardinal points, encloses two ambulatories on columns and
piers with bare ceilings and a central cylinder topped by a dome.
The cylinder's size is determined by the smallest circle that can enclose the rugged outline of a craggy rock. The exact shape of the
rock's surface in the late seventh century is not known, although it
is unlikely that it was smoother then than it is now. The cavern un-

der the rock could be entered through a small passageway just to the east of the southern axis. It is even easy to imagine how the building would have been used—as a place for circumambulation around a hallowed spot, entered and exited through any of its four doors. In this simplistic interpretation, all that remains to be done is to define the nature of the central spot's holiness and to identify from the practices of the Muslim faith the ceremonies or actions that could have been performed there.

In reality, however, the building is not as simple as it appears, and its possible uses are not so easy to define. The Dome of the Rock was certainly not designed for prayer, the most clearly identifiable Muslim act of piety in the seventh century, since it had no designated direction and relatively little space for the faithful to gather. Furthermore, no clear-cut and obvious association was made at that time between the Rock and some specific holy memory. Even circumambulation was problematic, as people would have been entering and exiting simultaneously at every door. The liturgical practice of circumambulating the Ka'bah in Mecca had not yet acquired its canonical form, and if a relationship to that holy city was desired, it would have certainly led to an open-air circumambulation for large masses of people, not an enclosed one for a few.

The plan of the Dome of the Rock also has peculiarities that demand explanation. One is that the two ambulatories are of different widths. Another is that the sets of columns in the circular arcade are not symmetrical but are all a few centimeters off from what their geometrically correct location would have been. The first anomaly was explained over a century ago as being the result of a very elaborate geometric composition (Fig. 25). It begins with two crossed squares set at right angles to each other inscribed in the circle around the rock. These squares are then prolonged until they meet and form the circle of the octagonal arcade. Squares inscribed within this second circle lead in the same way to the outer octagonal wall. The elevation of the central cupola is determined by another square based on the diameter of the rotunda that reaches the base of the dome, and the height of the dome is the square root of the same diameter.

More recent investigations, done independently by French (Marcel Ecochard), Russian (Sergei Hmelnitskij), and Israeli (Doron Chen) scholars, have improved on these drawings and have included the elevation of the building in their calculations. These analyses have established that the basic module of construction was a cubit of 0.3089 meters and that, in both plan and elevation, the composition of the building was based on the irrational proportions of the Golden Mean, which, since the construction of the Parthenon in the fifth century BCE, have been perceived as being conducive to aesthetic pleasure. In short, the Dome of the Rock was very carefully designed by architects well trained in the elaboration of geometric proportions.

But within this carefully conceived geometric grid, the architects introduced variations intended to produce two visual effects. One is to allow the viewer, regardless of which entrance he uses, to see all the way through the building and to be aware of a sequence of architectural panels in front of him that lead the eye to the outside.

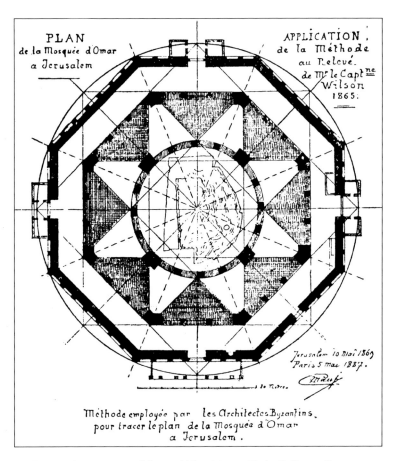

25. Geometric structure of dome. (After Mauss; K. A. C. Creswell; Ashmolean Museum, Oxford.)

Visually, the visitor is not invited to move around the building but to look through it. The second visual effect is more mysterious. Visitors entering the building are aware of a central empty space with a powerful central beam of light shining down from above. The light moves continuously, changing direction with the hours of the day, but the windows of the drum and the dome itself are invisible from most of the building. The octagonal arcade, with its eight triple gates, honors the center, leading visitors toward it through a series of screens, but the dome is not meant to be seen from the interior. It is prominent only as part of the building's exterior design.

Decoration

If the structure of the building is its architectural skeleton, with musculature suggested by the interplay of light and passageways, the astonishing decoration of the Dome of the Rock can be thought of as its exquisite skin. On the exterior, this skin was often repaired and restored, especially in the sixteenth and twentieth centuries, as we will see in Chapter 4. In trying to imagine how the building appeared in the seventh century, we must rely exclusively on descriptions by travelers or chroniclers and on a small number of archaeological documents. From them we learn that the lower part of the exterior walls was almost certainly faced with marble panels, and the only unanswerable question is whether the choice and location of individual panels formed a simply ornamental or perhaps an iconographic pattern.

The upper part of the walls and the parapet above them were decorated with mosaics that remained intact, to some extent, until the sixteenth century. Minor fragments discovered during various restorations can be seen today in the Haram Museum located on the southwest corner of the esplanade. The subject matter of this mosaic decoration is a bit of a puzzle. Such descriptions as we have from before 1300 do not say anything about their subject, and the fragments we possess show only geometric ornament, with perhaps a leaf or two. On the other hand, the many mostly Western Christian references that exist from the fifteenth and sixteenth centuries speak of representations of "cherubim," trees (often with precisely identified species), and even "palaces and ciboria" (small circular edifices often found in Roman painting). Since none of the writers involved had actually seen the building firsthand, they based their conclusions on distant perceptions or on what they were told by the local population.

Decorative trees and other forms of vegetation abound inside the building, and our chroniclers may have simply extrapolated their presence to the outside. Cherubim or anything looking like cherubim were never part of the decoration of the Dome of the Rock. But since, according to the Bible, they were represented on the facade of Solomon's Temple, these fictive elements could have been easily added to the description of something that these writers never actually saw.

The inclusion of palaces and ciboria is more peculiar, since such edifices are in fact found in the early Islamic mosaics of the Great Mosque in Damascus and are part of a standard vocabulary of Late

Antique art particularly common on the mosaic floors of churches from the seventh and eighth centuries in Palestine and Jordan. In contrast to the cherubim, which were certainly not there, architectural ensembles are theoretically possible and, as we shall see later, could fit with one of the explanations of the imagery of the Dome of the Rock. Yet I remain skeptical about their existence, because the sources for this information are late and foreign to the area and because no other evidence exists for the representation of architectural elements on the exterior of buildings. However enticing these many alternative hypotheses may be, the upper part of the walls on the outside of the Dome of the Rock was probably adorned with geometric and vegetal patterns. And indeed, the very fact of such ornamentation on the exterior of a building is original enough in Late Antique architecture to require an explanation.

The interior, by contrast, is a festival of decoration. In addition to the bronze plaques on the tie-beams of the octagon and the capitals of the columns, faint traces of paint can be seen on the wooden beams of the ceilings of the octagon. The inside surface of the outer wall and the eight piers of the octagonal arcade are covered with marble panels, sometimes beautifully carved, at other times chosen for their natural figure. Smaller marble plaques are carefully installed on the arches of the circular arcade. Since marble plaques could be moved easily from one area to the other or replaced when worn out, it is not possible to determine whether the current distribution of these marble pieces reflects some original pattern, perhaps an ornamental one. But if the specifics are uncertain, the general effect is clear to any visitor: a continuously fluctuating pattern of light moves around the room as rays from the windows above strike first one marble panel and then another over the course of the day.

The most spectacular feature of the building's decoration consists in its approximately 1,200 square meters of mosaics, the largest preserved program of wall mosaics anywhere in the Mediterranean area from before the twelfth century. Often repaired in past centuries and thoroughly cleaned and restored in the 1960s, the mosaics are, for the most part, in remarkably good condition on both sides of the octagonal arcade and on the piers and spandrels of the circular arcade. They have been heavily restored in the lower drum, although the composition of the original designs has been maintained nearly everywhere. Only in the upper part of the drum, in the area between the windows, have repairs and restorations altered the original patterns and simplified motifs into dry imitations of the earlier creations (Fig. 26).

Traditionally, these mosaics have been presented in two ways. One can be called sentence-like in the sense that a number of completed units of composition are identified and explained. The other way can be called phonetic, or possibly morphemic, as it consists of lists of elements, repeated or unique, found on the walls. Both ways are useful because they lead to different kinds of conclusions. The first emphasizes the impression that the mosaics make on the visitor; the second illuminates the vocabulary available to the artisan who executed the work. After outlining the main features of both approaches and introducing the inscriptions that adorn the upper part of the octagon on both sides, I shall propose a third ap-

26. Late mosaic pattern in upper drum, southeast area. (Saïd Nuseibeh.)

proach that derives from the first two and leads to what I believe is a deeper appreciation of the building.

Six different kinds of interior surfaces are adorned with mosaics. The first ones are square and rectangular surfaces on piers (Fig. 27). In almost all cases a large acanthus bowl gives rise to two thick bands that spread in volutes, often around a central rod. Many of the square or rectangular surfaces facing the center of the building also contain crowns, tiaras, necklaces, or other types of body jewelry. In one case (the northwestern pier), a vase replaces the acanthus bowl.

The second kind of interior surface consists of narrow elongated spaces (Fig. 28). The mosaics on all of these surfaces are organized around trees (often clearly identifiable palm trees heavily laden with dates) or around artificial compositions of leaves and stems arising from a vase, with jewels hanging on the stems as on a Christmas tree. Some trees have fairly naturalistic trunks, while others have trunks covered with jewels.

The third and most visible kind of mosaic surface consists of triangular areas over the columns of the octagonal arcade (Fig. 29). In nearly all instances, vases in the narrowest part of the space just above the columns exude totally artificial combinations of vegetal stems and leaves. On the face of the arcade directed toward the center, this vegetation is incrusted with crowns, tiaras, necklaces, and other items of jewelry, but never on the other side facing the outer wall.

The outer spandrels of the circular arcade, although comparable in shape to the triangles of the octagonal arcade, are the fourth

27. Detail of mosaics on rectangular surfaces of octagonal arcade, outer side in eastern area. (Saïd Nuseibeh.)

28. Mosaic with palm tree on long and narrow surface of octagonal arcade, inner face east side. (Saïd Nuseibeh.)

kind of surface that is decorated with mosaics—in this case, simple patterns of vegetal scrolls coming out of vases or acanthus heads or else imaginative constructions of artificial plants (Fig. 30).

A fifth surface is found on the drums, where neatly delineated rectangular units of vegetal scrolls emerge from a stunning variety of highly bejeweled vases with ornamental disks and pairs of wings

29. Triangular surfaces above piers of octagonal arcade, inner face east and southeast sides. (Saïd Nuseibeh.)

30. Mosaics on outer spandrel of octagonal arcade, northestern area.
(Saïd Nuseibeh.)

around a fruitlike center (Fig. 31). The very damaged spaces between the windows in the drum appear for the most part to be
poor copies of compositions similar to those on the drum below;
one of them is totally devoid of vegetal elements.

Finally, a sixth kind of surface is created by the soffits of the
arches in the octagonal arcade, and they are all different from one
another (Fig. 32). Each soffit is divided into three unequal segments, one occupying half of the available space and filled with a

31. Segment of mosaic decoration on the drum. Part of the Ayyubid inscription can be seen at the bottom. (Saïd Nuseibeh.)

32. Mosaics on soffits of octagonal arcade, eastern and southeastern area. (Saïd Nuseibeh.)

stunning variety of vegetal compositions comprising a unique array of motifs. A second segment is usually either a vegetal scroll or a sequence of circles and half-circles. And a third segment, the one facing the interior of the building, consists of decorated circles that continue onto the vertical face of the octagon and serve as a border to the designs found there. In other words, this segment does not operate simply as the decoration of a soffit but functions as a kind of hinge in the viewer's perception of the building's entire mosaic program.

Much has been written about the vocabulary of these mosaic compositions. It is relatively easy to enumerate the components: acanthus bowls of several different shapes; scrolls made of calices fitted into one another, occasionally simplified into a single ribbon with jewels and adaptable to almost any space; supporting rods, usually artificial combinations of repeated floral or ornamental elements; trees, among which palm trees can be recognized, and tufts of grass; garlands and single leaves which, especially on the soffits, serve as background for fruits; berries, fruits, and vegetables, among which pomegranates, olives, cherries, dates, grapes, and several kinds of cucumbers can be recognized; full or empty cornucopias of many different forms; vases; shells; crescents and stars; an astounding array of insignia associated with royal power, such as crowns or tiaras, and other jewelry of many kinds with no royal association; pairs of wings; and artificial combinations of several of these elements to create imaginative and fantastic compositions. Most of these types of decoration are found throughout the building except for the jewels and wings, which occur only on areas facing the center of the building. But it is possible that a more thorough and more systematic examination would unearth some other peculiarities in the location and arrangement of these motifs.

Whether discussing the mosaics as compositional types or as individual motifs, most scholars have concentrated on the origins and sources of these designs. The mosaics of the Dome of the Rock are of unusually high quality, and their motifs derive from a rich vocabulary of Antique and Late Antique decoration that existed all over the Mediterranean area, to which was added a few eastern (presumably Persian Sasanian) elements such as the pairs of wings and perhaps some of the composite trees. Considering the immense artistic activity of the seventh and eighth centuries in Byzantium, Egypt, Syria, Palestine, and Jordan, not to speak of Central Asia and the Buddhist world, we should not be surprised at the presence in an imperial and presumably well-funded creation in Jerusalem of so many elegant and sophisticated designs. The problem lies in reconstructing their meanings and what those meanings can tell us about why the building was built.

The main inscription on both sides of the uppermost part of the octagonal arcade is 240 meters long. The script is a very handsome angular Kufic known from several other Umayyad official monuments. It contains a few diacritical marks, but its full paleographic analysis is still to be made. Its text consists of excerpts from the Qur'an set between pious formulas and invocations. Since the question whether a complete text of the Holy Scripture was available at the time of the Dome of the Rock's construction is still debated, and since the process whereby texts from many different *surahs* of the holy book were selected is hard to imagine, in the discussion that follows I will present the inscription as a single continuous text, identifying in italics those segments found in the Qur'an and leaving aside their importance for the study of the scripture itself. The inscription begins on the outer face of the south side of the octagon and runs as follows:

Outer face: "In the name of God, the Compassionate, the Merciful, there is no God but God, One, without associate. *Say He is God, alone, God the eternal. He does not beget nor is He begotten and there is no one like Him* (Q 112). Muhammad is the envoy of God, may God bless him. In the name of God, the Compassionate, the Merciful, there is no God but God, One, without associate. Muhammad is the envoy of God. *Indeed God and His angels bless the Prophet. O you who believe send blessings on him and salute him with full salutation* (Q 33:56). In the name of God, the Compassionate, the Merciful, there is no God but God, One. *Praise to God who begets no son and who has no associate in power and who has no surrogate for [protection from] humiliations and magnify His greatness* (Q 17:111). Muhammad is the envoy of God, may God bless him and his angels and his envoys and peace unto him and the mercy of God, One and without associate. *To Him is dominion and to Him is praise; He gives life or death and He has power over all things* (combination of Q 64:1 and 57:2). Muhammad is the envoy of God, may God bless him and grant his intercession on the day of resurrection for his community. In the name of God, the Compassionate, the Merciful, there is no God but God, One without Associate. Muhammad is the envoy of God, God bless him." Then follows the foundation inscription which was discussed earlier.

Inner face: "In the name of God, the Compassionate, the Merciful, there is no God but God, One, without associate. *To Him is dominion and to Him is praise, He gives life or death and He has power over all things* (Q 64:1 and 57:2). Muhammad is the servant of God and His envoy. Verily God and His angels send blessings to the

Prophet. *O you who believe send blessings on him and salute him with full salutation* (Q 33:54). May God bless him and peace upon him and the mercy of God. *O people of the Book, do not go beyond the bounds of your religion and do not say about God except the truth. Indeed the Messiah Jesus son of Mary was an envoy of God and his word he bestowed on her as well as a spirit from him. So believe in God and in his envoys and do not say 'three'; desist, it is better for you. For indeed God is one God, glory be to Him that He should have a son. To Him belong what is in heaven and what is on earth and it is sufficient for Him to be a guardian. The Messiah does not disdain to be a servant of God, nor do the angels nearest [to him]. Those who disdain serving him and who are arrogant, He will gather all to Himself* (Q 4:171–172). Bless your envoy and your servant Jesus son of Mary *and peace upon him on the day of birth and on the day of death and on the day he is raised up again. This is Jesus son of Mary. It is a word of truth in which they doubt. It is not for God to take a son. Glory be to him when He decrees a thing. He only says 'be' and it is. Indeed God is my lord and your lord. Therefore serve Him, this is the straight path* (Q 19:33–36). *God bears witness that there is no God but He, [as do] the angels and those wise in justice. There is no God but He, the all-mighty, the all-wise. Indeed the religion of God is Islam. Those who were given the Book did not dissent except after knowledge came to them [and they became] envious of each other. Whosoever disbelieves in the signs of God, indeed God is swift in reckoning* (Q 3:18–19)."

This long text is a key element in any explanation of the purposes of the Dome of the Rock. But its importance does not lie solely in the meanings it conveys. The inscription is also an essential vector in the building, in the sense that it establishes a clockwise movement from the south to the west and ending up in the south again, if one begins with the outer face of the octagon, and a counterclockwise movement if one follows the inscription from the inner face. What creates this movement is not the possibility of actually reading the inscriptions, which is not easy to accomplish unless the sun or some other light is directed on it. It is the formal sequence of the longitudinal and vertical strokes of Arabic writing that provides the movement. This vectorial quality may be connected to another detail of the mosaic decoration, which is that the gold and mother of pearl cubes of the vegetal motifs are all set at a slight angle to the surface. The brilliant designs catch the light and shine out against the darkness of the background.

The interior of the Dome of the Rock appears, then, as a series of shining designs, the perception of which follows a movement of the eye compelled by the very shape of the building and by the movement of the sun's light through the windows. What that eye sees is a parade of jewels hanging on vegetation or a succession of white pearls and gold dots, both set against a much more static core of mosaics on the central drum, with their symmetrically arranged and fairly repetitive designs on a continuous background. In the building's interior composition, the octagon is the preeminent architectural feature, somber on its outer face and scintillating toward the center.

Other early inscriptions can be found on the exterior of this very talkative building. Two, hammered on bronze plaques, have

33. The bronze plaque originally at the eastern entrance, now in the Haram Museum and very much damaged in recent years.

been preserved from what was probably a set of four located above the entrances to the building; they were still hanging there until the restorations of the 1960s, when they were removed to the Haram Museum (Fig. 33). The inscription on the north gate goes as follows:

"In the name of God, the Compassionate, the Merciful, *praise be to God except whom there is no God, the living, the everlasting* (Q 2:255 or 3:1). There is no partner to Him, One, *unique He does not beget nor is He begotten and there is none like Him* (Q 112). Muhammad is the servant of God and His envoy, *whom He sent with guidance and the religion of truth to proclaim it over all religions, even though the polytheists hate it* (Q 9:33 or 61:9). Let us believe in God and what was revealed to Muhammad and *in what was given to the prophets from their lord; we made no difference between one and the other and we are Muslims to Him* (Q 2:139 or 3:78, slightly modified). God bless Muhammad, His servant and His prophet, and

peace be upon him and the mercy of God, His grace, His forgiveness, and His pleasure." There follows a rather long statement that
the inscription was ordered by the Abbasid caliph al-Ma'mun in
831, but these lines are written in a different script and were clearly
added later, probably replacing an earlier Umayyad inscription.

The second one, on the east gate, has the following text: "In the
name of God, the Compassionate, the Merciful, *praise be to God
except whom there is no God, the living, the everlasting, the creator
of heaven and of earth, and the light of heaven and of earth* (parts of
Q 2:255, 3:1, or 6:101), the Upholder of heaven and earth, *One,
unique, He does not beget nor is He begotten and there is none like
Him* (Q 112 minus one word), One, *lord of power, You give power to
whom You please and You take away power from whomever You
please* (Q 3:26). All power is to You and comes from You, our Master, and it returns to You, Master of power, Merciful, Compassionate. *He has written mercy for Himself, His mercy extends to all things*
(Q 6:12 and 7:156). Glory to Him and may He be exalted over what
polytheists associate [with Him]. We ask You, our God, by Your
mercy, by Your beautiful names, by Your noble face, by Your immense power, by Your perfect word by which heaven and earth
stand together and by which, and with Your mercy, we are preserved from the devil and we are all saved from Your punishment
on the day of the resurrection, by Your abundant grace, by Your
great nobility, by Your clemency, Your power, Your forgiveness, and
Your kindness, that You bless Muhammad, Your servant and Your
prophet, and that You accept his intercession for his community.
May God bless him and give him peace and the mercy of God."

The inscription ends with the mention of the Abbasid caliph al-Ma'mun and the date 831. Just as with the inscription on the north door, these lines are considered to be replacements for references to 'Abd al-Malik or later additions to an Umayyad text, contemporary with the construction of the building.

In all likelihood, given the symmetry that pervades the Dome of the Rock, panels with inscriptions originally appeared on the southern and western gates as well. A panel on the western gate is mentioned in twelfth-century sources, and the name of the caliph al-Ma'mun was misread on it by an earlier Persian traveler. No references to inscriptions on the southern entrance have survived, and it is just possible that no inscription ever existed. The southern gate faces the *qiblah*, or direction of prayer, and for this reason may have had symbolic and practical functions different from those of the other three gates.

Interpretations

These, then, are the architectural components that were brought together in the Dome of the Rock around 691. Interpretations of their meaning can be derived from two kinds of evidence: from formal sources and their implications; and from the iconography of the mosaics and the implications of the plan.

Much has been written about the architectural and decorative models that might have been used by the builders of the Dome of the Rock. And indeed one can point to earlier buildings whose shape is closely related. But no single monument has been identified as an exact prototype, and no known religious or secular structure of the seventh or even sixth centuries was decorated with the lavishness and brilliance of the Dome of the Rock. Of course, the existing record of pre-Islamic monuments is very spotty, often consisting of ruined churches and secular buildings whose ornamentation is usually long gone. Written sources, while occasionally useful, rarely provide the precision needed to answer scholarly questions, nor do they exhibit the synthetic approach of architectural criticism. They prefer approximate descriptions and make choices in what they see or know in order to fit some other rhetorical purpose. With no immediate model for the Dome of the Rock and no written document describing it at completion, all we can do is to locate the building within a visual language and then try to understand what that language is trying to say in this particular case.

I will deal separately with the structure and decoration of the monument, primarily because this corresponds to the separate ways in which builders and artisans operated. Patrons may well have thought in more synthetic terms, but their thought processes can only be imagined. Builders and artisans must stick to practical possibilities, which are far easier to reconstruct.

The phonetics of the Dome of the Rock—its piers, columns, capitals, semicircular arches, wooden dome, walls, doors, and windows—all belong to an architectural language that was common throughout the eastern Mediterranean world at the height of the Roman Empire and continued under Christian rulers for several centuries. Most of these elements were probably used and reused in the vicinity of Jerusalem, where a sizable labor force specializing in construction had been in residence since the time of Constantine and Helena in the fourth century. By the seventh century, the large space at the city's southeastern corner was full of discarded architectural fragments from Herodian and Roman times, and the Persian invasion of 614 must have left many Christian sanctuaries in ruins as well.

But if the phonetics of the building's language are easily explained, its plan and elevation are not, and the complicated problems they pose have exercised scholars since the late nineteenth century. The lack of well-preserved monuments from this period makes it impossible to assess the originality of the elevation. The plan, on the other hand—a circular or polygonal vaulted (usually domed) structure—belongs to a type with a long history going back to Roman mausoleums and pagan sanctuaries. In almost all known cases, the purpose of the building was to commemorate a person, a divinity, or an event. The earliest still-standing building whose composition and impact are related to the Dome of the Rock is a mausoleum on the outskirts of Rome that was turned into the church known today as Santa Constanza. A ring of columns in the center of the building supports the dome and creates an ambulatory around an empty middle.

In many variants, this building type became common for Christian religious martyria—monuments commemorating holy men and women or holy events—and for regular liturgical purposes as well. It was used for the Anastasis of the Holy Sepulcher in Jerusalem, the place honoring the burial and resurrection of Christ. And in the church of the Ascension on the Mount of Olives, datable to the fourth century CE, a large octagonal enclosure surrounded two circular arcades (Fig. 34). An equally thick outside wall is found in the octagonal church erected over the so-called Tomb of the Virgin in the fifth century, this time with a single circular arcade inside. The type can be seen in a church dedicated to Mary Theotokos on Mount Gerizim near present-day Nablus in Palestine, in a sixth-century cathedral in the southern Syrian city of Busra, and even as far west as Spain, where a large (22 meters in diameter) octagonal mausoleum with an inner octagonal arcade was discovered at Las Vegas de Pueblanueva, dated to early Christian times. In imperial Byzantine architecture, the type appears in the sixth-century church of San Vitale in Ravenna, itself a model for Charlemagne's early ninth-century palace church in Aachen in Germany.

It is thus easy enough to argue that the plan of the Dome of the Rock derived from a type of building used in Christian architecture to commemorate a person or an event, that the type existed throughout Syria and Palestine, and that it was already present in Jerusalem. But since few of the known examples are still standing and since often, as with the Holy Sepulcher, their elevation has been modified over the centuries, reconstructing them as they would have existed when the Dome of the Rock was being built is rather more difficult. Altogether, the simplest conclusion may be that the plan and elevation of the Dome of the Rock were adaptations of a common Antique and Late Antique architectural type to a terrain with its own constraints, including a large protruding rock.

But the discoveries in relatively recent times of three unusual examples of pre-Islamic octagons in Palestine may provide more specific and suggestive explanations for the form of the Dome of the Rock. These buildings have in fact been proposed as more immediate models than the general type. One of these buildings is found in Capernaum, located to the north of Lake Tiberias. This small town is mostly known for the ruins of a probably fourth-century synagogue with a later mosaic floor of Jewish symbols, depicted in a rude, folksy style and often reproduced in surveys of Jewish art. Less well-known is an octagonal building, just a block away from the synagogue, measuring some 16 meters in diameter, which has been excavated and studied by several archaeological teams since its discovery in 1968 (Fig. 35). Five of its sides are faced with a portico whose floor was covered with a repetitive, ruglike mosaic design. The other three sides, on the eastern section of the building, were abutted by common rooms of unknown purpose; a baptistery was added later.

In the center of the building, a smaller octagon (7.90 meters in diameter) surrounds a mosaic floor consisting of an all-over pattern of circles with a peacock in the middle. No trace has been found of an altar, and the latest interpretation of the building is that it commemorated the whole area's association with St. Peter, whose original house may have been on the site, near a synagogue in which Jesus preached. The preservation of the synagogue as a restricted Jewish place of worship may have required Christians to erect the octagonal building to commemorate a memory that was historically located in the still-functioning Jewish synagogue

34. Schematic reconstructed plan of
the church of the Ascension on the
Mount of Olives.

35. Schematic plan of Capernaum.
(After V. Corbo.)

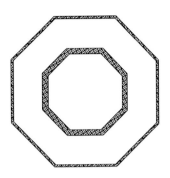

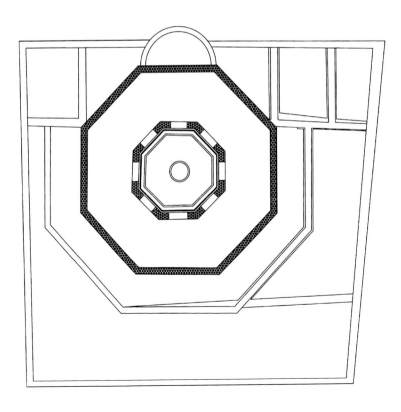

nearby. We can only speculate on the ways in which this new building would have been used, but for our purposes what matters is that an octagonal form was chosen to deal with an unusual holy or cultic need.

A second Palestinian example is (or rather was) far more spectacular. At the beautiful site of Caesarea, by the Mediterranean, Herod the Great erected a large platform for a Roman temple whose facade faced the sea—a stunning sight, no doubt, for incoming travelers. Apparently no traces of that temple have survived, except for columns and capitals strewn around the ruins. But in the sixth century an octagonal building was constructed more or less in the center of the platform (Fig. 36). The building was some 39 meters in width and contained an inner octagon presumably bearing a high dome. The reconstruction proposed by archaeologists bears a close resemblance to the Dome of the Rock, in part because the excavators used the Jerusalem monument to imagine the elevation of a building they could know only from rather pitiful remains. But even granted the hypothetical nature of the elevation, there is no doubt about the plan and dimensions of the building. And the location of the octagon on a high platform makes for a striking composition, just as with the Dome of the Rock.

But what exactly was this building? It had no apse and therefore was not a typical congregational church. The most likely explanation is that it was a central-plan martyrium. But who was the martyr, or what was the event, that would have justified such a visually important location? The persecution of only minor Christian fig-

36. Schematic plan of an octagonal building in Caesarea. (After K. G. Holum.)

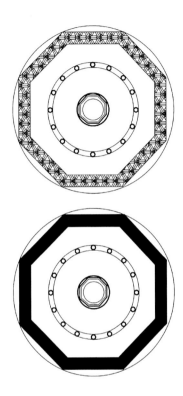

ures is associated with Caesarea, which was an administrative center and pleasure retreat for the rich and powerful rather than a major urban center. And contemporary or later written sources do not mention a spectacular martyrium in the city. In theory at least, the octagonal building could have been a secular pavilion, public or private. The matter may eventually be resolved archaeologically or otherwise. Again, what matters to us is the use of a simple geometric program of two octagons for some purpose that entailed a brilliant awareness of urban space. Like the Dome of the Rock in Jerusalem, the monument on the Caesarea Herodian platform was a beacon, intended to be seen as well as used.

My third example is, at first glance, the closest to the Dome of the Rock in shape as well as in type and location. Some ten years ago, a very curious church was accidentally discovered a few miles from Jerusalem on the way to Bethlehem, near a Greek Orthodox monastery. It consists of an octagon some 13 meters wide around a largely empty area with an irregular rocky outcrop in the center (Fig. 37). An octagonal ambulatory, whose floor was decorated with mosaics, surrounds the first octagon, and a second octagonal zone comprises what has been identified as four small chapels with mosaic floors. A large apse on the east side clearly indicates that the structure served as a regular church, beyond whatever functions were fulfilled by the small chapels. The church has been identified as the one built in the middle of the fifth century by Juvenal, the first patriarch of Jerusalem, and dedicated to the Kathisma or "Seat" of the Virgin, to which two apocryphal traditions are connected: a place where the pregnant Mary stopped to rest on the way to Bethlehem, and a place where she paused during the later escape to Egypt with Joseph and the child Jesus.

In Christian religious practice after the fifth century, the significance of this church, which commemorated rest stops that were not described in the Gospels, was downplayed, to the benefit of Bethlehem and its connection with Joseph's descent from David. But the church remained, even though pilgrims rarely mentioned

37. Schematic plan of the church of the Kathisma of the Virgin, near Jerusalem. (After R. Avner.)

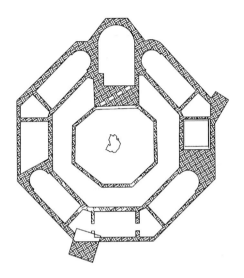

it. In the early seventh century, probably after the Muslim takeover of the area, it was restored, and one of its new mosaic floors shows a palm tree remarkably similar to one of the mosaic trees on the wall of the Dome of the Rock. Further, the Dome of the Rock's inscription gives particular importance to Mary in its statement about Christianity, and the palm tree under which she rested is part of the Muslim message. An archaeologist involved in the excavation of the church has even argued that the church was transformed into a mosque in the early Islamic period. Good arguments can be made against this transformation, but whether it happened or not, we can say with certainty that the size of the building, its design, the presence of a rock in the middle, possibly the importance of Mary in the Qur'anic message, and perhaps parallels in decorative designs relate the church of the Kathisma of the Virgin to the Dome of the Rock.

I hesitate, however, to propose that the church served as a model. One reason is that the points of comparison between the two buildings are easily offset by differences, such as the existence of an apse in the church, its small chapels, and a completely different organization of space. Another reason is some doubt whether, by the late seventh century, the Qur'anic passages dealing with Mary had been localized into specific places of commemoration, if not worship. While Mary is indeed present in the inscription of the Umayyad building, she is a minor element, and I have difficulty imagining that the Muslim designers of the Dome of the Rock sought inspiration in a building of secondary importance within their Christian environment.

What all three of these examples suggest, however, is that the octagon and its variations, however ubiquitous the shape may have been, was used whenever some unusual purpose was meant for a building beyond the obvious commemorative function. The octagon seems to have been an architect's answer to an unusual commission. This could be so because of the easy way in which variants can be incorporated into the basic type. The Dome of the Rock would represent the type in its purest and simplest form, and its lack of significant modifications and additions indicates a purpose for which there was no model. The building was also meant to be seen from afar, and as an architectural object it had secular associations with power and pleasure, as well as religious ones.

Yet, the most important point I wish to make is that the explanation I propose is not a historically genetic one, leading from a specific monument to another specific monument with such mutations as may have been required by individual needs. It is rather an interpretation involving a typology of forms—an argument that certain forms seem to lend themselves to certain uses, and not just because they were previously used in a similar way. This methodological distinction is of some importance in understanding and defining the formation of Islamic art—and perhaps in the development of any art.

In addition to these parallels between the architecture of the Dome of the Rock and that of comparable buildings, what can we learn from the interior decoration about the building's original purpose and meaning? Because the mosaic program dates for the most part to the time of the building's founding in 691, we can view it as an original document or "text" reflecting choices made and purposes defined in the late seventh century by the patrons themselves—the caliph 'Abd al-Malik and his circle of advisers, especially Rajah ibn Haywah and Yazid ibn Salam, the men in charge of construction. Furthermore, by the nature of its complex designs adapted to the different surfaces provided by the architecture and thus comparable to but different from one another, the mosaic decoration lends itself to iconographic and programmatic interpretations because of the variants in similar motifs or because of the location of some motifs.

In a sense, the mosaic decoration resembles the main inscription (presumably designed and executed by the same teams of planners and craftsmen) in that it seems repetitive without really being so and its variants over established models are neither obvious nor visible without some effort. And, like the terms of the inscription, the details of the decoration can be seen individually only if one focuses on minute particulars; but just as the inscription provides a visual border to the building's decoration, the mosaic program is more immediately effective as a lush field of colors and shapes than as the sum of individual motifs.

Much has been written about the meaning of these motifs, picked for the most part from a rich vocabulary of Late Antique architectural decoration in the Mediterranean area. And even the pairs of wings and artificially constructed trees, from the Iranian Late Antique, may have already been included within the Mediterranean vocabulary before the coming of Islam, according to recent research on the mosaics of Saloniki in Greece. For some features of these mosaics—the vegetables on some of the soffits or some of the jewels and crowns—no immediate parallel exists, as they do for so many scrolls, acanthus compositions, cornucopias, or trees. Whether these were invented for the Dome of the Rock or have hitherto undiscovered parallels, they belong to the same visual language.

Although this is impossible to demonstrate, the mosaicists who worked on the Dome of the Rock probably were not imported from Byzantium, as they may well have been for the slightly later mosaic decoration of the Great Mosque in Damascus (the matter is the subject of some scholarly debate). Plenty of evidence from mosaic floors suggests a high level of craftsmanship in Palestine and what is now the Kingdom of Jordan during the seventh and especially eighth centuries. Wall mosaics are rarer today than floors because they were much more expensive to execute in the first place and because few buildings have survived with their walls intact. But a high level of technology and craftsmanship was certainly available in Jerusalem for wall mosaics, as it was for floors. An interesting detail confirms both the effort put into the decoration and the expectation that the work would be rapidly completed. Several of the soffits of arches I was able to study some forty years ago have a symmetric design along a single axis at the apex of the arch. In most cases, one half of the decoration is better executed than the other half. This suggests that master craftsmen provided a design which was then copied by apprentices.

No contemporary or later written sources describe or explain the decoration of the Dome of the Rock. In fact, beyond acknowledging the brilliance of the decoration and the quality of the marble panels set over the lower part of the walls, written sources are totally silent on the themes illustrated by the mosaics, in striking contrast to the details provided about columns and capitals and to the interpretations given in medieval texts of the mosaics in the Great Mosque in Damascus. Several explanations can account for this silence. The main one is probably that the decoration of the Dome of the Rock never demanded a semantic meaning in the same way that other early Islamic buildings like the Damascus mosque did, because the building was not an easily accessible public monument.

So what meanings do these mosaics have? Three broad answers

can be proposed. One is that the decoration was simply ornament, a beautifying feature without deep iconographic or symbolic significance. This "positivist" interpretation is exemplified in
Marguerite van Berchem's thorough analysis of the mosaics attached to K. A. C. Creswell's description of the building. It fits with
the conception, long dominant in some scholarly circles, of an
aniconic early Islamic culture that liked to show off its affluence
with the use of an expensive decorative technique and to display its
taste in the choice of motifs but which did not endow the designs
with any particular meaning other than aesthetic pleasure and the
soothing attraction of sophisticated combinations of subjects artfully covering architectural surfaces.

In this view, the mosaics of the Dome of the Rock would be our
earliest example of what Lisa Golombek has called the "draped
universe" of Islamic art. We can admire and analyze the ways in
which the decoration of soffits leads from one octagon to the
other, and scrolls spread to cover large rectangular spaces, while
different trees fill vertical areas. And as a striking additional benefit
to the visual experience, the side of the octagonal arcade that faces
inward is adorned with crowns, tiaras, and jewels of all sorts (Fig.
38). These are all beautiful things set in gold or mother-of-pearl at
a slight angle from the surface of the wall, like a garland on a tree,
installed to catch the light from the sun or from hundreds of candles hung all over the building. The outer side of the octagon does
not have the same brilliance, and only one spandrel is provided
with jewels. Was it a later repair by someone who no longer understood the visual point of the decoration, or was it a technical mistake from the time of the building's creation?

38. Interior view over the Rock; note the opening over the cave.

The brilliance of the face of the inner octagon directed toward the center of the building found a fascinating parallel in the outside mosaic decoration facing the city of Jerusalem and its surroundings. Too little has remained of this decoration to permit any reconstruction of the designs made for these mosaics, but they certainly had a colorful effect that could be seen from afar—unique, so far as we know, in the Mediterranean area. The only comparison was the Ka'bah in Mecca, a roughly cubical sanctuary which in the seventh century was covered every year with a different cloth of many colors, providing a pre-Islamic Arabian background to the notion of a "draped universe" for sacred places and holy buildings. Only much later was the scheme we see today—a black cloth with an inscription woven in gold—adopted for the Ka'bah.

We shall see that this parallel may explain some of the impact made by the Dome of the Rock. But in the case of the Ka'bah, as with the positivist view of the Dome of the Rock, apparently no symbolic or iconographic meaning was attached to the decoration of the monuments. The visual or aesthetic parallel between the two buildings may well explain why, as early as the ninth century, Muslim written sources, usually Shi'ite ones deeply hostile to the memory of the Umayyad caliphate, claimed that the Dome of the Rock was built by 'Abd al-Malik to replace the Ka'bah and to move the obligatory Muslim pilgrimage (the *hajj*) from Mecca to Jerusalem. This interpretation persisted in some Muslim circles and was accepted by quite a few contemporary scholars of Islamic culture. Many arguments lead us to reject it on historical grounds, not the least of which being that 'Abd al-Malik was too wise a ruler to go against a basic obligation of the faith. But a visual and even aesthetic relationship between the two buildings is a legitimate conclusion to draw.

Without denying the accuracy and the partial validity of a positivist and essentially aesthetic interpretation of this decoration, two additional or alternative layers of meaning must be considered. One, initially developed by me almost half a century ago, took as its point of departure the inscription of the octagon. It singled out the Christological content of the inscription and its proclamation of Islam as the final revelation of a divine message already present in Judaism and Christianity. It saw the Dome of the Rock as a monument celebrating in the Christian city *par excellence* the victory of the new faith and its creation of a new holy place on an area full of memories and abandoned, if not desecrated, by the Christians. ʿAbd al-Malik and his advisers were probably aware of the Jewish significance of the site, but the inscription does not allude to it at all. The crowns and the insignia of the decoration, on the other hand, would have been the insignia of the rulers and lands defeated by Islam, and they were hung like an offering in a holy place.

Once again, the Kaʿbah in Mecca is where we find symbols of defeated opponents and other religious or secular movements. The horns of the ram sacrificed by Abraham were found there, and these horns were said to have been hanging for a while in the Dome of the Rock before being returned to Mecca. In short, some features in the decoration of the Dome of the Rock can indeed be interpreted as reflections of a political event, the takeover and reconsecration by Muslims of a Jewish holy memory in a Christian city. The purpose of the decoration would have been to strengthen that message by associating the representation of symbols of defeated rulers with a religious text proclaiming Christ as a prophet before Muhammad and inviting the local population to accept this third and last form of divine revelation—Islam.

Another interpretation was first developed by Priscilla Soucek and then elaborated by Miriam Rosen-Ayalon and especially Raya Shani, who put together its latest and most coherent version. She calls it the "iconography" of the Dome of the Rock, because she explains the themes of decoration in terms of a coherent program representing clear and precise items. The term is misleading, because actual representations, symbols, and visual evocations are mixed together within this scheme. I prefer to call this interpretation "religious," because, far deeper than the previous one, it deals with aspects of Muslim beliefs and practices and seems directed almost exclusively toward a Muslim public. Yet, this interpretation is no more than a hypothesis, as we are still very poorly informed about the formation and dissemination of these beliefs.

Two components stand out in a "religious" interpretation of the decoration and logic of the whole building. The first component is the Solomonic one. Mount Moriah has always been the site associated with Solomon's Temple and, by an extension current in popular rather than learned sources, with Solomon's luxurious palace built by the jinns and visited by the Queen of Sheba in a dramatic narrative often embellished in Jewish, Muslim, and Christian sources. The most direct parallels are with features from the

Temple, as with the conches on the soffits of the octagonal arcade, the cornucopias intertwined like horns and recalling the Jewish liturgical *shofar,* or the bejeweled trees and other forms of vegetation that appear in post-Biblical descriptions of the Temple and palace. Raya Shani further notes that the possible Solomonic references are particularly striking on the western side of the octagon, thus implying an awareness of the layout of the Jewish Temple, whose altar would have been located on the rock inside the building. It has even been suggested that the location of motifs like horns (which can be associated with Solomon) between Sasanian and Byzantine crowns evoked the two destructions of the Jewish Temple by the Assyrians, who were assimilated to Persians, and by the Romans whose heirs were the Byzantines.

Without doubt, Solomonic associations for the Dome of the Rock and for the Haram in general were made by Muslim writers in later times. And one of 'Abd al-Malik's sons who became caliph for a few years (715–717) and was active in the war against Byzantium and in building new cities like Ramleh, the new capital of Palestine, was named Suleyman; he may have had dreams of being a new Solomon. But Solomonic associations within the Muslim community at the time of the building's construction are almost impossible to imagine. The tradition *(hadith),* allegedly going back to the Prophet, that 'Abd al-Malik announced the eventual resacralization of the Jewish Temple is certainly an invention of later times. Most significantly, our one authentic contemporary text— the main inscription on the octagon itself—makes no reference to Solomon nor to anything connected with the buildings that had been on the Haram. One cannot exclude Solomonic evocations, primarily palatial ones, in the rich vegetation depicted on the walls of the Dome of the Rock, because Solomon was certainly present in the memories associated with Mount Moriah. But it is difficult to conclude that these evocations were the primary subject matter of the decoration. Such an interpretation requires the involvement of secular patrons in pre-Islamic sacred history to a far greater extent than can be imagined for the Umayyad ruling circle.

We can be much more positive about the second "religious" aspect of the decoration, which does have a striking confirmation in the inscriptions, especially the one on the eastern door of the building. Visually, a program of real or imaginary trees and vegetal scrolls as well as the presence of jewels everywhere, and even the range of crowns and other insignia of power and wealth, can all be connected with Paradise, the eternal and beautiful garden so frequently depicted or evoked in the Qur'an and in the parallel eschatological visions of Christianity and Judaism. A vision of Paradise is particularly meaningful in Jerusalem in the last decades of the seventh century. Jerusalem was to be the site of the Resurrection, which would begin on the Mount of Olives and in the ravine separating it from the city proper. This had been an area of tombs for many centuries, and all three monotheistic faiths were ripe with announcements of the end of time, the coming of the Messiah, and the beginning of the divine judgment. Eventually the Muslim tradition would locate on the Haram or in areas to the east of the city many of the places where specific moments in the high drama of the last days were expected to take place. The setting is unlikely to have developed by 691 in all of its later details, but the theme of the end of time and the beginning of eternity was certainly present in the late seventh century.

Two written texts confirm this. One is the inscription on the east door of the Dome of the Rock itself, which proclaims the power of God "which passes all understanding" (as it is put in Christian liturgical practice, taking over a passage in a Pauline epistle) and which blesses Muhammad, the prophet and servant of God, because he provides the intercession between sinful man and the divine justice to come. This characteristic of Muhammad may well explain why, in the long inscription of the octagon, the Prophet's name is repeated so frequently and his continuing role is contrasted with the completed role of Jesus. In 'Abd al-Malik's time, on coins and on inscriptions and probably in pious life altogether, the definition of Muhammad's place in the formal proclamation of the Muslim profession of faith was being firmly established. On coins his presence expressed the power of the newly united commonwealth, and in the Dome of the Rock he was invoked as the intercessor for men and women at the dreaded moment of divine judgment.

A second text, discovered and analyzed by Josef van Ess, makes it possible to move yet one step further, even though the document itself is not dated. According to an early tradition later rejected by Muslim theologians but current in Syria before the end of the eighth century, when Muhammad was taken on his Night Journey *(isra')* from Mecca to the "farthest mosque" *(masjid al-aqsa)* in Jerusalem, he stopped first at the grave of Abraham in Hebron, then at the place of Jesus' birth in Bethlehem, and then at the Rock in Jerusalem. There, his leader, the archangel Gabriel, said to him: "Here your Lord ascended to heaven." The traces of feet on the Rock would have been the traces of God's presence on earth at the time of creation. This account, accepted in the late seventh century, may have led to the inference—in parallel with Christian eschatology—that this was also the place to which God would return at the last judgment.

With these bits and pieces of evidence from the time of 'Abd al-Malik or not more than a generation removed from it, we can propose the following explanation for why the Dome of the Rock was built, without searching for evidence in later texts or in later explanations of the building. It had the shape of a commemorative building, like nearly all known octagonal structures, and it was positioned to dominate not just a large, probably unfinished esplanade but the whole city and much of its surroundings. Many memories, emotions, or even practices were associated with it, but the ones that seem culturally and chronologically most likely to have inspired its construction were three. The main one was eschatology, the moment to come—soon, according to the mood of the times—when God would return to earth to judge men and women. He would appear at the place from which He left the earth at the time of creation, the Rock over which the Dome was built. His messenger on earth and the intercessor for the faithful was the Prophet Muhammad, who was honored and praised in the inscriptions of the building and who was the last of a prophetic tradition that included Abraham and especially Jesus (the list would grow over the centuries).

A second theme, after eschatology, was the Muslim victory over the Christian world and the takeover of the holy city of Jerusalem. Triumph expressed so as to be seen by all from everywhere in the city was a major feature of the Dome of the Rock. Another secondary theme was the brilliance of the Jewish Temple and of the palace built by Solomon, whose colorful gardens of vegetation covered with jewels decorated a monument related, if only symbolically, to the beautiful life to come in Paradise.

As Carolanne Mekeel-Matterson has proposed, the Dome of the Rock was a paradox: it was a commemorative building, a martyrium in Christian terms, and also, in Arabic and Muslim terms, a *mashhad*, meaning literally "a place of witnessing" for an event yet to come. Its purpose was unique, and no model for it existed; its patrons had to find ways to adapt building practices and decorative programs to fit these new purposes. None of the schemes for the building, neither the religious ones nor the imperial ones, were new, but they had never been put together in quite this way before. Once the impetus for the Dome of the Rock's creation lost its intensity, what was left was a stunning monument with an overwhelming aesthetic and visual power. It was also a building of such structural and decorative purity that it was very difficult to transform when new needs or different modes of behavior arose. Ideas and beliefs had to adapt to the building. The following four centuries would bring about that adaptation.

3 700 to 1100

The Completion of a Sanctuary

The city taken by the Crusaders in 1099 was quite different from the one flourishing around 700. The latter, which had kept more or less the same size and dimensions it had under Christian Byzantine rule, was dominated by two parallel rocky heights identified by their respective religious compounds. The one in the western part of the city was Christian; it included the extensive Holy Sepulcher complex, the Justinianic basilica of the Nea, and whatever remained of the sanctuaries on Mount Zion. The other compound, in the eastern half of the city, was Islamic; it centered on the shining new Dome of the Rock and probably the first Aqsa Mosque on a partly refurbished Herodian esplanade identified as the "mosque (*masjid*) of the Holy City."

To the south of the Haram, the Islamic sector also encompassed new settlements for immigrating Muslim Arabs and probably Jews returning after several centuries of absence from Jerusalem. Considerable intermingling of families with different religious observances had taken place, and while a representative of the provincial governor and a police or military force was probably present, we have no evidence that such authorities were very active. Most likely, each community operated by itself, and some sort of collective consensus governed the city. The sorts of struggles and turmoil that had shaken the Islamic community in the 670s and 680s probably no longer affected the physical city after 690. From that time until the Crusades, its inhabitants seem to have enjoyed relative peace.

The Jerusalem of 1099 was somewhat smaller than the eighth-century city because a large bulge that had extended it to the south during the reign of the Byzantine empress Eudocia had been abandoned. The Holy Sepulcher had also shrunk in size during an early eleventh-century reconstruction. And even though the number of pilgrims arriving singly or in groups from Latin Christendom seems to have increased during that century, many churches were abandoned by 1099 for lack of support. The Muslim population was no longer concentrated to the south of the Haram but had spread to the north and the northwest. The sizeable Jewish community that had settled in the city over the centuries could not claim a distinctive quarter, but its religious and secular institutions extended from inside the walls to the Mount of Olives.

A remarkable feature of the city between 700 and 1099 is that each of the three religions with spiritual or liturgical connections to Jerusalem was represented by several sects. Among Muslims there were Sunnis belonging to different schools of jurisprudence, Shi'ites of various persuasions, and sufis—individual mystics for the most part who occasionally organized themselves into groups. Karaite and rabbinical Jews could be found, along with—among

Christians—Chalcedonians, the mainstream Greek or Latin faithful, and many smaller heterodox, monophysite, or Jacobite congregations. While frequent and at times violent conflicts between confessional sects occurred, antagonisms among the three major religious groups rarely flared.

Over the course of these four centuries, Jerusalem would attract many individual men and women from lands as far away as Ireland and the Indus valley, as well as members of religious sects and many Jews, but it was at best a weak magnet for outsiders. One reason was the city's location off the main routes of trade, and its lack of significant economic output of its own. Mecca shared these characteristics, but by the beginning of the eighth century that urban center had already acquired an exclusively Muslim spiritual and ritual position that no other city could approach. Mecca's historical and symbolic message to Muslims was clear and precise, backed by a proper set of scriptural injunctions in the Qur'an. By contrast, Jerusalem at that time had no clearly stated and spatially specific function in Muslim piety, and its major Muslim monument—having arisen from a complex and confusing set of practical and ideological causes—had not received collective acceptance or approval within the Muslim community of the faithful (*ummah*). Christians and even Jews had a similarly restricted and, at that time, ill-formulated relationship to the city.

What would happen between 700 and 1100 was the transformation of the Dome of the Rock into a concretely focused Muslim holy place within the context of a newly recognized sacred space, eventually to become known as the Haram al-Sharif (Noble Sanctuary). During that time, Muslims would slowly change the name of the city itself from Iliya (the Arabization of the Roman administrative term Ilium) to Bayt al-Maqdis (the House of Holiness or of the Temple) and then to Al-Quds (Holiness), the name it carries in the Muslim world today.

No consistent or coherent picture of Jerusalem from these centuries has come down to us. References to the city occur in the major chronicles written in Baghdad or later in Cairo, but they are rarely systematic and contain, to my knowledge, no mention of the Dome of the Rock or the pious functions of Jerusalem. Far more fruitful are the texts by writers loosely called geographers, a vague category that included bureaucrats making descriptions of the Muslim world for the administration in Baghdad, travelers describing their impressions and adventures for remote audiences, and litterateurs collecting information about exotic lands and pious practices for their encyclopedias of knowledge.

One of these traveling officials was Shams al-Din al-Maqdisi (often, if incorrectly, known as al-Muqaddasi), a man of great curiosity and intelligence who knew a lot about the whole Muslim empire, and even about matters beyond the empire's boundaries. Born in 946 in Jerusalem, he spent much of his adult life outside the city; and like many testimonies by native sons, his description of the city is often more important for its sentimental values than for its accuracy. The most original of the so-called geographers was Nasir-i Khosro, a Persian philosopher and poet. He belonged to the Ismaili sect led by the Fatimid caliphs in Cairo, and he was an acknowledged agent of their power. His *Sefername* (Travel Book), with its description of Jerusalem in 1047, reads at times like a social scientist's report, based on carefully kept notes, observations, and possibly drawings. Precisely because he came from elsewhere and was writing to evoke the character of a very specific place for a distant audience, his account is particularly trustworthy.

In the tenth century a new literary genre appeared, the *Fada'il* (Praises), which concentrated exclusively on Jerusalem and on particular spaces in the city with religious associations. These *Fada'il* are invaluable for their definition of the pious and historical mythology that had developed around Jerusalem by the end of the first millennium. They are less reliable as sources for a purely factual political history of the city or its buildings; and, curiously enough, they are remarkably uninformative about the monuments themselves. Like many historians or theologians of our own time, the authors of these books were blind to or uninterested in the physical configuration of the city they praised. Jerusalem was for them an abstraction full of stories, not a constructed space with visual indicators of history, piety, or behavior.

And finally we have archaeological and visual records of repairs and renovations, occasionally of additions and novelties. These modifications are preserved in inscriptions, sometimes in textual references, much more rarely in eyewitness accounts of construction or decoration. Further investigations may eventually provide additional bits of evidence about these architectural alterations and embellishments.

From all of these sources, we can conclude that the four centuries between the completion of the Dome of the Rock and the arrival of the Crusaders turned out to be more important for the meanings that accrued around the Dome of the Rock than for any changes in the form of the monument itself. Accordingly, I have divided the available information into two broad sections. First, I will identify, more or less in chronological order, the events or activities that affected the Dome of the Rock, or could have done so, and for which we possess reasonably clear evidence. I will stress in particular the development of a visual context for the building—a group of structures and other objects intended to strengthen and emphasize its impact. I will then jump to the middle of the eleventh century and to Nasir-i Khosro's account of Jerusalem and its monuments. Using this account in parallel with the geographies of the preceding century and the nearly contemporary *Fada'il,* I will sketch out what the Dome of the Rock seems to have meant to educated Muslims a generation before the arrival of the Crusaders. And in conclusion I will propose a more hypothetical explanation of the changes in meaning, if not in form, that affected, sometimes permanently, this architectural masterpiece of the late seventh century.

Visual Context

Like any work of architecture, the Dome of the Rock was in constant need of repairs from natural or man-made damage and of alterations to meet new needs, new tastes, or special occasions. Some of these activities have been recorded in inscriptions left on the building, and a few are mentioned in geographical or historical texts. But most of them were probably unnoticed by contemporary observers and were recorded in administrative documents that no longer exist.

In the early years of the Abbasid caliphate, the route taken by the caliphs from Baghdad to Mecca passed occasionally through Jerusalem. Thus, in 758 and 771 al-Mansur, the founder of Baghdad, visited Jerusalem on his way to or from the Arabian peninsula, as did al-Mahdi in 780, Harun al-Rashid a few years later, and possibly al-Ma'mun some time during his long reign (813–833). It is difficult to imagine that al-Ma'mun would have ordered that his name replace that of 'Abd al-Malik in the central inscription of the Dome of the Rock without having seen the building. But we cannot be sure, because by al-Ma'mun's time the well-endowed direct road from Iraq to Mecca across the Arabian desert—the *darb Zubaydah*—was functioning and allowed travelers to bypass the ancient southward route through Syria and Palestine.

With one exception, no specific work on the Dome of the Rock is known from the early Abbasid period. The one exception is a set of inscriptions dated 913–914 and located on the beams of the wooden ceiling over the inner octagonal ambulatory. These inscriptions probably record some repairs or restorations in the ceiling, done under the direction of one Labid, client of the mother of the caliph al-Muqtadir, according to Max van Berchem. They are among the earliest evidence for the patronage of holy places by women, though what they reflect is no doubt piety rather than power.

While the Abbasid caliphs did not make major changes in the

Dome of the Rock itself, they did sponsor transformations in the covered hall *(mughatta)* on the south side of the Haram. By siting what would eventually become the Aqsa Mosque on the same axis as the Dome of the Rock and giving it a dome of its own to indicate the location of the mihrab, the early Abbasids strengthened the visual connection between these two major buildings on the esplanade, or possibly they simply completed a connection that had begun under the Umayyads. Some of the steps leading up to the central platform were probably constructed at this time, especially the southern set and the main western one, but the exact history of these means of access to the platform will not be known without further archaeological investigation.

During the ninth and tenth centuries, Palestine was dominated politically by Egypt and the upstart dynasties of the Tulunids (868–905) and the Ikhshidids (935–969), who paid only nominal obedience to the Abbasid caliphs in Baghdad. Almost nothing is known of their architectural activities in Jerusalem or near the Dome of the Rock, but one historical detail that left no archaeological trace may be of some significance for understanding the meaning of the monument during these centuries. This detail is the burial of several Ikhshidid leaders in Jerusalem, to the east of the platform on which the Dome of the Rock sits, even though none had died there. The old Jewish, and to a lesser extent Christian, feeling that a burial in Jerusalem carried some advantage in the rewards of the afterlife seems to have appeared within Islam's religious ethic around this time. It is interesting that the best-known expression of this belief came from a dynasty of converted black slaves in Egypt.

The second half of the tenth century was a time of major political and cultural change for Jerusalem and particularly for the Dome of the Rock. In 969 a dynasty of Shi'ite caliphs claiming descent from the Prophet through his daughter Fatimah took control of Egypt and founded the city of Cairo. The ambition of these Fatimids was to replace the Abbasid caliphate of Baghdad. They planned to accomplish this succession by establishing more or less continuous sovereignty over Palestine, Syria, and the Arabian peninsula, supporting all sorts of subversive movements throughout the Muslim world, and asserting control over the holy cities of Mecca, Medina, and Jerusalem. Jerusalem was under Fatimid control from 970 to 1070, when a Turkmen military chieftain took over in the name of the new Turkish leadership that was assuming power over most of the eastern Islamic world.

The Fatimid century was relatively peaceful in and around Jerusalem. The city was only indirectly affected by a few Beduin revolts in 1011–1014 and 1024–1029 and by the Fatimid struggle with an extremist movement of Qarmatians, who prevented the Fatimids from taking control of the holy cities of Arabia. Two events stand out as having major effects on Jerusalem during this time. One occurred in the first decade of the eleventh century, when the mentally deranged caliph al-Hakim, intent on persecuting Jews and especially Christians, nearly destroyed the church of the Holy Sepulcher in 1009 and looted its treasures. The second was a severe earthquake in 1038 that damaged the esplanade and many of its monuments. A major program of reconstruction followed these events: the Holy Sepulcher was rebuilt, though smaller in size and less forcefully visible; the walls of the city were shortened to correspond more or less to the walls we see today, a task completed by 1054; and the Aqsa Mosque was rebuilt and redecorated. On a triumphal arch in front of its dome, a beautiful mosaic inscription, still preserved, proclaimed the work of the caliph al-Aziz in 1035 and, for the first time in Jerusalem, copied Qur'an 17:1, the verse that mentions the Prophet's journey from Mecca's Masjid al-Haram to the *masjid al-aqsa*, "the farthest mosque," by then fully acknowledged to have been in Jerusalem.

In short, the Fatimid period saw significant physical, ideological, and spiritual changes in Jerusalem, some imposed by political events and others the result of a natural disaster. Fatimid activities and investment in Jerusalem probably grew out of an ill-focused attempt to transform the city into a major pan-Islamic sanctuary, in as much as the dynasty never managed to wrest full control of the holy cities in Arabia. These policies had several effects on the Dome of the Rock. A major reconstruction of the building's dome took place in 1022–1023 and again in 1027–1028, by order of the caliph al-Zahir. This work was recorded in three (originally probably four) carefully carved inscriptions invisible from both the inside and outside of the building. They were placed between the two layers of the domes, just above the drum, on the cardinal points of the building. The inscriptions could be reached by climbing a stairwell on the southeast area of the dome and walking through a small passageway that ran between the two layers of the dome. (I do not know whether they are still accessible.)

The exact nature of the repairs is not known but may have included most of the interior of the cupola and the mosaics of the upper and lower drum, whose dry and simplified style is so strikingly different from seventh-century decoration. Repairs may also have included the exterior mosaics, which today are largely gone. Eventually a careful analysis of tesserae and of designs will permit students to separate the different phases of decoration and repairs from one another. A single, probably only fragmentary, inscription has remained on the upper part of the western side of the drum, which provides the date of 418 AH (1027–1028 CE) for repairs of these mosaics (Fig. 39). The extent of the area affected by these restorations cannot be determined at this stage of our knowledge, but the fact that the inscription is preceded by the conjunction "and" *(waw)* suggests that more than one restored area was identified.

What matters about the repairs for our purposes is the implication of the invisible inscriptions inside the dome that record them. They begin with the first seven words of Qur'an 9:18: *"Verily the sanctuaries of God will be maintained by those who believe in God."* This verse is commonly quoted in its entirety in mosques throughout the Muslim world, as it continues with a list of a believer's basic obligations. In this instance, the part could have been meant for the whole, according to the practice known in many representational arts whereby only a segment of a complete visual statement needs to be shown in order to transmit the message. Or else, as a

39. Mosaic inscription in lower drum, dated 1027–1028. (Saïd Nuseibeh.)

finite quotation, it was meant to invoke divine favor for those who restore buildings dedicated to God.

This last explanation is probably the right one, especially if one considers that the statement was repeated at the four cardinal points, thus adding a cosmic aura to the caliph's action, and in places invisible to visitors. The upkeep of the sanctuary was an act of piety favored by heaven and dedicated to God alone, not formally for the benefit of the faithful. The Dome of the Rock was thus acknowledged as a sanctuary whose maintenance was the ruler's responsibility. Nothing was said about the purpose of the building, but the ending of the inscription was a prayer expressing the expectation of the patron: "May God give glory and power to our lord, the Commander of the Faithful, may He give him the possession of the East and of the West of the earth, and may He find him worthy of praise at the beginning and at the end of his actions."

The difference between al-Ma'mun's simple appropriation of a building sponsored by someone else many years earlier and al-Zahir's use of the sanctuary as an intermediary with God for his earthly ambitions is striking, as is the fact that al-Zahir hid his statement from public view, in contrast to al-Ma'mun, who made his statement visible to all. The Fatimid caliph's message was directed to God alone, although he may have included public inscriptions in several places on the drum's interior.

A final curious innovation attributed to the late ninth century was the installation of a mihrab inside the cavern under the Rock itself. The panel involved was once thought to be late seventh century and therefore the earliest preserved mihrab, even though it was flat rather than concave, as the earliest mihrabs were supposed to have been (Fig. 40). This early dating is no longer accepted, but the mihrab does pose a set of curious problems. It is odd that nothing is said in the oldest available sources about the interior of the Rock, in contrast to the many stories and myths explicating its surface. The only myth to be eventually, and probably fairly early, associated with the cavern is that it resulted from the Rock's attempt to follow the Prophet when he ascended into heaven. But it was held back by the hand of the Prophet, whose fingerprints on the surface were much later identified.

The flat mihrab was not carved out of the Rock itself but fixed to the wall of the cavern. It was originally of white marble and belongs, typologically, to a relatively small group of objects of comparable size which have a thick and heavily decorated arch set over twisted columns, and writing along the borders and in the middle. The inscription on the border of the Rock's panel is too damaged to be read, but the profession of faith ("There is no God but God and Muhammad is His Prophet") is carved on a lintel within the arch. The quality of the design and the details are not of the highest order, and the late tenth-century date proposed for it is possible, perhaps even likely, but not established. Why this plaque was put in the cavern is a bit of a mystery. A simple reason would be to indicate the proper direction for prayer in a dark space. But who prayed in this minuscule enclosure under the Rock? Why would the need for a plaque have arisen in the late ninth century, two hundred years after the construction of the Dome of the Rock?

40. The so-called "mihrab" located under the Rock. Its date is unknown but usually given as eleventh century.

And why is the design of the plaque so unsophisticated, when the quality of most of the decoration in the building is remarkably high?

The answer to these questions may well be that no significance was attributed to the cavern until long after the building of the dome. The traditional collective prayer of Muslim pious practice that is usually associated with a mihrab is unlikely to have taken place in this small space. The mihrab can, however, be associated with private, individual prayer, a theme of much importance in Islamic Jerusalem at this time, as we will see. Perhaps all flat mihrabs were meant for restricted private use, or possibly they were funerary symbols, since death and resurrection were constant themes in the piety of Jerusalem. Too little is known about the existence and meaning of symbols in early Islam to consider this possibility as anything more than a hypothesis. But since we know of a long-standing tradition of Christian and Jewish visual signs associating Jerusalem with resurrection, the possibility of a similar phenomenon in Islam cannot be excluded.

Another and even more mysterious feature to appear at this time is the Black Paving Stone *(balata al-sawda)*—a stone located in the northern part of the octagon that was of a different hue from others. On that spot, pilgrims or visitors were expected to recite a celebrated prayer beginning with "O Lord I take refuge with you," which, according to Muslim tradition, the Prophet uttered with his companions when they came to Mecca. Initially, this stone probably just happened to be of a different color. But in a spirit typical of the Holy Land since early Christian times, any unusual feature in nature or in the works of man could be connected with a pious memory; and, if necessary, that memory could be invented. The Black Paving Stone was not mentioned by many writers or visitors, and it is no longer apparent today.

These repairs or additions to the Dome of the Rock have two characteristics in common. One is the care given to a recognized but ill-defined sanctuary by the ruling establishment of the Islamic world, whether in Damascus, Baghdad, Fustat, or Cairo. The second is the appearance of features that suggest a new use for the building in popular piety that had almost nothing to do with its original intent. We shall see shortly that all these features can, however tentatively, be tied into a broader system of meaning.

In addition to repairs and renovations, the visual context of the Dome of the Rock was transformed by other structures on the platform where it stood. We do not know the history or the chronology of the changes that occurred there, but by, say, the year 1000 the platform had acquired on its edges a low wall of green marble with incrustations of stones of different colors, and six sets of stairs led up to it (Fig. 41). In most descriptive writing these steps were called *darajat,* the proper name for stairs, but pious texts and inscriptions call them *qantarahs* (bridges) or *maqams* (emplacements) for notable events, translated a bit audaciously as "ascents" by a recent writer. The various names reflect tensions between descriptive, pious, and perhaps secular values that characterized much of Jerusalem at that time.

To the south was the maqam of the Prophet, which faced the entrance to the Aqsa Mosque and was associated with the Prophet's

41. The platform of the Dome of the Rock, seen from the east. (Israel Images / Alamy.)

arrival in Jerusalem. To the east of the mosque and always on its south side was the maqam Ghuri, named after a Fatimid official who sponsored a particularly striking ensemble of three sets of stairs ascending from three different directions and an arcade on top of the platform whose beautiful mosaic inscription gives the sponsor's name. The location of this maqam on the side of the

Haram farthest from the city, and at a time when the southern gates of the Haram no longer provided major access to the esplanade, is a bit of a puzzle. It may have been connected to ceremonial practices peculiar to the Fatimid period, which favored external expressions of power and piety that did not survive the dynasty's demise.

Of the two western stairways, one was associated with the mysterious Muslim prophet al-Khidr, who, invisibly it is said, prayed there every day. The stairway to the north was unusually large, perhaps to reflect the northern gate to the Haram, known as the Gate of Gates *(bab al-abwab)*, but perhaps also to accommodate the growing Muslim population to the north of the Haram.

How the specific locations of these stairways were determined escapes us today, as none of them is on axis with either the Dome of the Rock or the Aqsa Mosque. Their design was also original in medieval and Islamic architecture in that they were topped by arcades of three or four arches supported by columns. This formal arrangement was unknown in Roman antiquity and was perhaps inspired by city gates or triumphal arches. Without doubt the arcades were meant to be honorific passages between the esplanade and the platform, but the question is whether they were passageways from the platform to the esplanade, from the esplanade to the platform, or both. The inscriptions that have been preserved are found on the side of the arcade facing the Dome of the Rock, suggesting to me that they greeted the pilgrim as he moved from the holiest part of the sanctuary to the less hallowed ones. But as is so often the case in Jerusalem, the opposite can be argued as well: the arcades and their inscriptions may have represented a set of visual signals oriented in the direction of the holiest place, in the same way that the most ornate mosaics inside the Dome of the Rock faced the center.

Thus the platform and its main sanctuary acquired a colorful enclosure, almost like a belt, which highlighted the sacred space. This enclosure within the larger esplanade was further sanctified by a set of small commemorative domed structures, all connected with the Ascension of the Prophet. Most of them were damaged by the Crusaders and reconstructed after 1200, and shifts of nomenclature since that time confuse their identification and obscure their histories. But wherever they were and whatever their original shape, they included the Dome of the Gathering (Qubbah al-Mahshar), where the prophet gathered for prayer all angels and prophets (a building that is not mentioned in late Fatimid descriptions); the Dome of the Prophet (Qubbah al-Nabi) north of the Dome of the Rock, where the prophet prayed alone; the Dome of the Ascension (Qubbah al-Mi'raj), whence the Prophet ascended into heaven; and the Dome of Gabriel, where Gabriel prayed and where Buraq, the steed that carried the Prophet, waited.

Was there a master plan behind the arrangement of structures on the Haram, in a city that had no significant political power and was far removed from centers of religious authority like Baghdad or Cairo? What role did the Dome of the Rock play in such a plan, if there was one, and how did the immediate decisions made by a host of individual artisans factor into its execution? To begin to answer these questions, what matters first is that these domes all appeared under the Fatimids in the tenth century; and second, that they all have some association with the Night Journey and the Ascension of the Prophet, events which at that time were not yet connected specifically with the Dome of the Rock and were absent from all early accounts of the building in Jerusalem. It is as though a new wave of popular piety was moving toward its eventual harbor but had not reached it yet—a mighty wave of eschatological hopes, historical or religious associations, and political power washing over a building that had been endowed originally with very different values.

This phenomenon of a building whose meanings and forms have different histories is rare, if not unique. One of its most touching expressions occurs in Abu Muhammad 'Abd Allah ibn Muhammad al-Hawli's dream of a visit to Jerusalem on the night of August 10, 946, as recorded by Ibn al-Murajja, an author of one of the *Praises:* "The Gate of Mercy is, from the side of the mosque [the west] a gate made of light, but from the side of the valley, a gate made of iron [a reference to Qur'an 57:13 identifying a wall separating mercy from punishment]. The Hitta Gate [on the north side of the esplanade] is the Qur'anic gate concerning which God has ordered 'Enter this gate doing obeisance and say "hitta," and we shall forgive you your transgressions' [Qur'an 2:58] and everyone who enters this gate or descends to it becomes as free of sin as he was on the day of his birth. Making ritual prayer at the Birthplace of Jesus and at the Chamber of Zachariah [located in the southeastern corner of the Haram] is like entering Paradise, entering these places is like looking at Mary and Jesus or at Zachariah and Jesus. From the [south] gate of the Dome of the Rock to the Copper Gate [the Aqsa Mosque] are trees of light and a path of light as white as snow; the trees are explained as the way the faithful go with God, as opposed to the blocked ways of their opponents, and the path of light is white because this was the way of Muhammad on the night of the Night Journey.

"The Dome of the Chain and the Chain after which it is named are said to be made of light and invisible to men. The place of the Dome [of the Ascension] glitters green and red like a rainbow. The Rock is a red ruby, and only some people are allowed to see it thus; from under the four sides of the Rock light is coming forth, these are the four rivers of Paradise; the Dome of the Rock has a large and high dome made of white light with a pearl on top. In the first row [presumably inside the Aqsa Mosque] people are swallowed up by the earth, with their heads sticking out; these are the people who hate their ancestors" (Andreas Kaplony, *The Haram of Jerusalem*, p. 75).

Leaving aside the last sentence, whose interpretation of divine punishment would take us far afield, we notice a remarkable feature about this tenth-century dream: that eschatology and the Prophet's mystical journey are deeply intertwined within the physical layout of the holy space. Furthermore, light and colors are everywhere and are especially striking as connectors between holy places. It is as though a pious dream had sought to interpret the colors and the brilliance of the Dome of the Rock by providing them with a new religious significance. And it is reasonable to ask whether the colorfulness of the Dome of the Rock and its surroundings, within an architectural practice that did not particularly favor color, was from the very beginning a willed attempt at providing visual expression to eschatological themes, or whether the interpretations followed, slowly, the presence of an unusually colorful architecture.

Meanings

A fleeting survey of a few preserved inscriptions, accidental text references, and a small number of recorded modifications or additions made to the fabric of the Dome of the Rock between 700 and 1000 sketch a hazy picture indeed. We can see that a striking building, carefully maintained in its pristine appearance, took on a host of new associations, as did its immediate surroundings, and inspired new acts of piety. But are we dealing with an evolution in the meanings ascribed to the monument over the course of these four centuries; and, if so, can we reconstruct a chronology of their appearance? By 1099, as the Crusaders approached, had a religious "story" been formally established in the Haram of Jerusalem that provided a new context for the Dome of the Rock?

To answer these questions, at least in part, we turn to a unique document, the *Travel Book* of the Persian philosopher and political activist Nasir-i Khosro. He was an official in the administrative district of Merv in the northeastern Iranian province of Khorasan, today in Turkmenistan, where he was born. He dabbled in verse and in esoteric philosophy and eventually became quite successful as a poet and a thinker. At some point in his life, he joined the Ismaili branch of Shi'ism, a sect at the peak of its power thanks largely to the successes and ambitions of the Fatimid dynasty in Egypt. In 1045 Nasir-i Khosro began a journey of seven years, probably connected with Ismaili missionary activities, that took him to Jerusalem, Cairo (where he spent some time and for which he provided a fascinating description), Mecca, and Medina, before he returned to the area of Merv. From there he was exiled to the remote province of Badkhashan in northeastern Afghanistan, where he died.

While in Merv, Nasir-i Khosro wrote up an account of his travels. We learn from it that he took notes during his trip which often included measurements of buildings and other places of historical or religious significance. In the case of Jerusalem's Haram, he wanted to get "a general idea of the plan and layout," and so for a long time he "wandered about the area, looking at it from different vantages" before making his measurements (Thackston translation, p. 30). When he found an inscription (probably the one recorded by the Swiss scholar Max van Berchem as no. 163) that gave the actual dimensions of the esplanade, he compared his own results—however he obtained them—with the archaeological record.

We can easily imagine Nasir-i Khosro as a medieval version of the gentleman-scholar-pilgrim so common among European Christians in the late nineteenth century. His attitude and practice in the field, and his objective of making an impression on readers in faraway lands, give a lot of credence to his descriptions. The comments he transcribed from conversations with local inhabitants have some of the flavor of contemporary anthropology.

Nasir-i Khosro will be our primary guide to eleventh-century Jerusalem. We will compare his statements to those of other writers from the tenth and eleventh centuries—geographers who described the Muslim world of their time under the title *Kitab al-Buldan*, Book of Lands—particularly two literary-minded Arabic authors. The first of these was Ibn al-Faqih, whose long text on Jerusalem was written in 905. He begins with the by then rich literature on the associations between the city and the prophets from Abraham to Muhammad and also with the Muslim conquest in the seventh century; of particular importance is his description of the Temple of Solomon. For all its piety, this first section—an accumulation of traditions and pseudo-historical information, with little critical thought—lacks spirituality or emotion except whenever the Last Judgment is mentioned. The second shorter part is a sort of statistical survey of structures on the Haram—how many columns, large stones, capitals, fountains, water jugs, and so on were there—along with a brief description of the Dome of the Rock as essentially the sum of its columns, piers, and domes.

The other geographer, Shams al-Din al-Maqdisi, mentioned earlier, was born in Jerusalem in 946 and remained a loyal Palestinian patriot, even though he traveled much in the eastern part of the Muslim empire. His descriptions of the monuments are more precise than Ibn al-Faqih's, and he brings an aesthetic rather than a mechanical sensibility to bear in his account, where the pious uses of structures on the Haram play a relatively minor role.

We will also compare Nasir-i Khosro's text to the new genre of *Praises*, particularly a book composed around 1020 by Abu Bakr

Muhammad ibn Ahmad al-Wasiti, who was a local gatherer of *hadith* (traditions) about the life of Muhammad, and another book written around 1030–1040 by al-Musharraf ibn al-Murajja al-Maqdisi, whose work contains, in addition to historical and mythical accounts, a great deal of information on the practices expected of pilgrims.

Nasir-i Khosro begins by describing the walled city as prosperous and well-populated with artisans. On its eastern side, beyond the Haram, is the space where the Resurrection will take place. People live in this area in order to be at the right place when the time comes. A large cemetery nearby (still standing today) includes fancy tombs from ancient times that fascinated our traveler. Further to the east was the valley of Gehenna—the valley leading to Hell. According to some local inhabitants, one can occasionally hear the voices of people in Hell; and like an obedient tourist, Nasir-i Khosro went to experience this for himself. But he could not hear anything. This note of skepticism (which much later will color Mark Twain's vivid account of the Holy Land) contrasts strikingly with the prayers for forgiveness the Persian traveler addressed to God.

Nasir-i Khosro relates that shortly before Moses' death, God commanded him to designate the Rock on the Haram as the direction of prayer. Then in Solomon's time a sanctuary *(masjid)* was built around the Rock, which remained the direction of prayer until the time of Muhammad, when it was replaced by Mecca. Thus, in a telescoping of history and myth, the holiness of the Haram derives from its being both the *qiblah* as propounded by Moses (who, in the Biblical narrative, never came to Jerusalem) and the site of Solomon's glorious building. The point of Nasir-i Khosro's visit was to participate in a host of holy associations made with this space between the time of Moses and Muhammad and to perform a number of actions, mostly prayers, not so much to honor these associations as to profit from their sanctity and to increase the spiritual value of his prayers for his own salvation.

Nasir-i Khosro entered the Haram from the west through a splendid gate. It stood high above a city that covered the Tyropoeon Valley, which was much lower then than it is now. The gate had been built by one of the Fatimid caliphs, probably al-Zahir, who reigned between 1021 and 1036. Located at the present Bab al-Silsilah, the main entrance to the Haram today, it was called then the Gate of David. Its two parallel wings were covered with domes and adorned with mosaics containing the name and title of the ruling Fatimid caliph. In tone and style, these inscriptions may have been similar to the majestic inscription on the triumphal arch of the Aqsa Mosque that also proclaimed the glory of the ruling Fatimid caliph. The doors themselves were of brass that gleamed like gold, and they were heavily decorated. Having been made aware of the place for the Resurrection on the other side of the sanctuary, Nasir-i Khosro entered the actual holy place through a space built and decorated by the ruler of his own time.

The great esplanade that the visitor entered was surrounded by a portico on its western and northern sides, of which only fragments remain today. The visitor then turned northward, and along the northern edge of the esplanade he found a dome supported by piers known as Jacob's Dome and another dome with a mihrab, identified by an inscription as the mihrab of the prophet Zachariah, who used to pray there, almost constantly, during his lifetime. Just outside the portico and the esplanade were cloisters (the Persian term *darvizeh* has many possible meanings) for individual mystics, with several handsome mihrabs, probably individual flat niches like the one found in the cavern under the Rock.

On the eastern wall was the structure known then and today as the Golden Gate—the place where God accepted David's repentance, a symbolically important gesture in the Qur'anic Revelation (38:22–25). The gate had been transformed into a mosque and was provided with beautiful carpets and a staff of its own—presumably readers, cleaners, lighters of candles, and so on. Nasir-i Khosro himself prayed at this double gate of repentance and mercy *(Rahmah wa Tawbah),* confessing his own sins. In the southeastern corner of the Haram, what is now known as the Cradle of Jesus was provided with an array of mihrabs recalling Mary and her father, the other Zachariah of holy history, and with appropriate inscriptions. On one of the columns of whatever was constructed there, traces could be seen of an indentation by two fingers, said to be those of Mary holding on to the column while in labor.

Finally, on the south side stood the renovated Aqsa Mosque, identified by Nasir-i Khosro as the place to which God brought Muhammad from Mecca. By then this was the definitive interpretation of Qur'an 17:1, whose text—"Blessed be He Who carried His servant by night from the Masjid al-Haram [Mecca] to the *masjid al-Aqsa* [the farthest mosque]"—is inscribed on the triumphal arch of the main nave of the mosque. Nasir-i Khosro describes the mosque at great length, and his description is often compared with al-Maqdisi's, written seventy-five years earlier, and with the modern building, whose central part is still the Fatimid structure seen by our Persian traveler. It is curious that, except for the Qur'anic citation, Nasir-i Khosro does not mention any historical or pious connections with this monument, which had been so recently restored. For him, the mosque was a building whose purposes and functions were clear; the only responsibility of a guide was to describe its constitutive elements and to praise the quality of its workmanship. Spatial or structural distinctions or differences in decorative style that so fascinate modern historians were of no significance to a religious visitor of the time.

While memories of the past do not appear in his descriptions of the building, they do surface when Nasir-i Khosro discusses the area under the mosque and its immediate surroundings. He attributes these substructures to Solomon, as was usually the case in the Middle Ages with nearly all of Herod's constructions. In the history of Jerusalem as told by Muslims, Herod's work and personality seem to have been forgotten. The underground passageways and the southern section of the esplanade are associated in Nasir-i Khosro's account with Muhammad, who entered Jerusalem through what is now known as the Double Gate located under the Aqsa Mosque. Muhammad's cousin Hamza left an impression of his shield on the masonry as he leaned against the wall—or at least this is Nasir-i Khosro's explanation for the probably Herodian decoration found there, which does indeed include ornamental panels in the shape of shields. He associates other southern gates with Jewish history and the passage of the Ark of the Covenant, which, at least in the Islamic statement of its fate, was taken to heaven by a host of angels.

Having thus walked around the whole of the esplanade, admired the renovated public mosque, prayed for forgiveness on the east side, seen mystical gatherings in the northeastern area, visited the places where Jesus was born and through which Muhammad came to Jerusalem, and having almost returned to the beginning of his circuit, Nasir-i Khosro next turned his attention to the central platform. (The term he uses is *dukkan*, a term more commonly used for furniture or objects.) There, he says, is the Rock, "which was the *qiblah* before the appearance of Islam," thus making a connection with an unspecified past, identified at the beginning of his account of Jerusalem as the time of Moses. The platform had to be built, he says, because the Rock was too high to be fitted under a simple roof. This explanation is preposterous, but it shows that the question of why the Dome of the Rock was built in the first place was asked and, as we will see, answered in several ways over the course of its history.

The platform was framed by a wall of marble and reached by six sets of stairs, which Nasir-i Khosro describes individually later in his account. It is clear from the importance he gives to the steps that they were part of a recent refurbishing of the whole Haram that any visitor would admire. It is also interesting that he mentions them in detail as he leaves the platform, thus supporting the interpretation I propose of an enclosed space defined by a colorful marble wall and a fancy set of gatelike passages that led visitors back to the more mundane world around that space.

Finally, Nasir-i Khosro moves to the Dome of the Rock itself and says, quite incorrectly in fact but obviously psychologically true, that the sanctuary sits in the middle of the platform, which is itself in the middle of the larger esplanade. His confused description of the Dome of the Rock can easily be explained by inaccurate or imprecise notes taken on the spot and expanded much later. He acknowledges the quality and the beauty of the piers, columns, and capitals, and he records the fact that the ceiling is covered with geometric designs and that the walls are ornate "beyond description"—a curious cop-out for someone who has measured so many walls and counted so many piers. The only artistic feature that elicits a comment is the numerous large silver lamps sent by the Fatimid rulers of Egypt. In a passage that smacks of political propaganda, he lets us know that even the candles of these lamps impress him. He does acknowledge traces of footprints on top of the Rock—which was by this time protected with a marble screen—and he attributes them to Abraham and Isaac. This pious visitor who mentions so many associations with holy history elsewhere in the Haram is curiously silent about memories of people and events mentioned by other writers. He refers to the Rock only as an early direction of prayer and does not see a need to explain why the building was maintained in such good shape and so well endowed with both attendants and devotees.

Three additional domed buildings are part of the constellation of structures on the platform, according to this account. To the east of the Dome of the Rock is the Dome of the Chain, whose invisible chain put up by David could only be reached by the sinless on the day of judgment. Here again, Nasir-i Khosro did not check his notes, or else he took them without observing the structure very carefully. He agrees that the Dome of the Chain was open on all sides except for the south side (facing Mecca), with its mihrab, but he claims that the dome was supported by eight columns and six piers, whereas in reality there were eleven columns and six piers. The numbers given by Nasir-i Khosro are more logical and easier to understand than the true ones, which have not been explained to this day.

To the northeast of the Dome of the Rock was the Dome of Gabriel, set on four marble columns and provided with a fine mihrab. There were no rugs, Nasir-i Khosro notes, perhaps because it was not meant to be a place of prayer. The dome simply identified the spot where the Prophet mounted his steed. Near it was the Dome of the Prophet, also resting on four columns. According to our guide, when the Prophet came out to ascend to heaven, the Rock rose up to follow him. The Prophet put his hand on the Rock and froze it in its place, half suspended in the air. Still today, a small domed reliquary-like object covers the place where, according to Muslim belief, the Prophet's fingers made an imprint on the Rock. In Nasir-i Khosro's time, the Prophet was thought to have embarked on his journey from the place where the dome that bears his name is sited.

If we restrict ourselves to visual appearances and pious functions, the other written sources of the tenth and eleventh centuries only add details to Nasir-i Khosro's descriptions. Ibn al-Faqih, like most authors of *Praises,* provides pages of associations made between Muslim and Jewish stories and the Dome of the Rock and its surroundings, mostly a wide range of Biblical accounts as transmitted by the Qur'an and other Muslim traditions or passed down through rich Jewish legends. The one Muslim event connected with the Rock is the Night Journey and Ascension of the Prophet. But the role of the Rock is that of a witness to the event; when the Rock tries to participate by following Muhammad, the Prophet restrains it. The ancient relationship of the area to the Last Judgment is still present, but it has clearly become secondary as the millenary expectations of the seventh and eighth centuries abated. All these accounts together combine to define the sanctity of the Holy Land in general and of Jerusalem in particular, more so than the holiness of any one particular building or urban space.

Most of these writers were engrossed with statistical documentation of the buildings of the Haram, especially the Dome of the Rock. Perhaps this reveals what we may call an accounting mentality, whereby quality and significance are determined by quantities of artifacts like columns or piers. It is not that piety is absent from these descriptions, but rather that Muslim piety as exemplified in Nasir-i Khosro's account is quite different from the traditional Christian piety that has defined so much of our conception of the term. Spaces may indeed be identified by their association with ancient events, actual or mythical ones; piety, however, does not consist in praising or reliving these events (as Christian pilgrims did, for example, in their visits to the Via Dolorosa in Jerusalem) but in presenting one's purified self to God through the action of prayer. Prayers in Islam are collective as well as individual, and the spaces in which they take place may increase their value. So many writers state that prayer in Jerusalem or on the Haram is worth more in the eyes of God than prayer elsewhere. In the absence of a liturgy performed by a clergy or of physical sacrifices, the pious act of the Muslim believer is a personal encounter with the divine through the formal gestures of prayer. The Haram in Jerusalem provides, at regular intervals and in places sanctified by commemorative associations, mihrabs—small flat ones for individuals, larger niches for groups—which designate the direction of prayer but, more profoundly, serve as foci of attention that prevent external interference in the act of devotion.

The remarkable feature of the Fatimid Haram in the eleventh century, as we can reconstruct it from these various sources, is that an old urban space which had accidentally become Muslim four hundred years earlier acquired a new form. Somewhere in the center an elevated platform of multicolored marble was accessible through fancy stairways. It was like a closed garden with four domed buildings, one of which dominated the entire city. The main dome was associated with God, the Revealer, who created the earth and would come again to judge men and women. But this vision of Paradise had, by the eleventh century, been filtered through the presence of the Prophet. In inscriptions of the late seventh century, Muhammad had been simply the intercessor between man and God at a time yet to come. But four hundred years later his intercession had become dramatized by the extraordinary Night

Journey and Ascension into heaven to see God and by the hierarchies of angels and prophets surrounding him as well as the horrors and pleasures of the world to come. This central platform is itself surrounded on three sides by the memories of various manifestations, over the centuries, of divine power, and on the western side (actually, for a while yet, the entire southwestern corner) by the living city under the control of the Fatimid caliphs, the sponsors and patrons of the holy space whose symbols and signs decorate most passageways.

Some recent writers have suggested that, from the Umayyad period onward, a formal master plan for the Haram, first imagined as early as the seventh century, was brought to fruition by the Fatimids in the first half of the eleventh century. The existence of such a plan is not very likely, given the architectural and urbanistic culture of the time, if for no other reason than that the sponsors of major work in Jerusalem always resided elsewhere, in Damascus, Baghdad, or Cairo. And yet two features of early Islamic architecture in this period more or less required architectural visualizations of some sort, that is, actual drawings or small-scale models or at the very least mental images of constructed spaces. One such feature was the hypostyle mosque that appeared in a consistent form from Spain to Central Asia and India. The other is the Masjid al-Haram in Mecca, where remote sponsors, mostly in Baghdad, created a unique sanctuary. The history of this complex still awaits its chronicler, but it is hard to imagine how it could have been built without plans, sketches, or models that traveled back and forth between Mecca and Baghdad. There are no drawings for Jerusalem's sanctuary known to me from the centuries before the Crusaders, as we have from the twelfth century onward. But such drawings were certainly possible once paper became a relatively inexpensive medium for the transmission of knowledge and information in the tenth century.

We can thus propose that by the middle of the eleventh century, a visually coherent space had been created on the Haram. It was surrounded by walls with elaborate gates and a colonnade on three sides. On the south end was a great mosque, nearer the middle was a special sacred platform with a domed building more or less in the center, and scattered around were various structures for commemoration or prayer. The chronology of the appearance of these buildings still escapes us for the most part. What is certain, however, is that the trek of the pilgrim at this time included private forms of pious behavior in addition to traditional collective prayer and the celebration of a few feasts. A pilgrim like Nasir-i Khosro observed a pattern of personal devotion which may well have been new in Muslim piety and which had interesting parallels with Christianity. At times these acts were performed separately from the official religious behavior common to all Muslim communities and could involve individual practices or group activities directed by some charismatic leader.

In Jerusalem, eschatological hope always remained in the forefront for all believers, regardless of their specific faith. But the true novelty in the Muslim faith of the eleventh century is the overwhelming importance accorded to the Prophet's mystical journey from Mecca to Jerusalem and then to heaven. All the new buildings were devoted to it, and the old buildings were given a role in the story. The Dome of the Rock itself played a secondary part, but over the following centuries it would appear at center stage again. The contrast between the visual impact of the Dome of the Rock and the relatively limited religious meanings associated with it at this time must have struck Nasir-i Khosro and led to the imprecision of his account of the building.

But we can move a step further in our reconstruction of the Dome of the Rock and its area in the eleventh century. Surrounded by a powerful natural setting of magnificent yellow to brown stones, the domes of the Haram, especially the two that towered over the Rock and the Aqsa Mosque, as well as some of the gates to the esplanade and the enclosure of the platform, were shining beacons to the faithful, both night and day, a most unusual feature in the area. Covered as it was with precious stones and gold, the Haram seemed to depict that future Jerusalem which appeared in Jewish legends about the end of time and in the Christian Book of Revelation. To the historian of art, the Haram combines in an extraordinary, perhaps unique, way a Herodian esplanade created in the first century BCE with buildings erected in the seventh century and later, which were transformed in the eleventh century into a coherent whole. This mix made particularly striking use of colorful mosaics, stones, and metals, of pious legends and myths covering a millennium, and of the ideological ambitions of Umayyad and Fatimid rulers. Few visitors, then or now, can be aware of all these elements at the same time. But their strength is that they created a work of art which demanded preservation.

4 1100 to 1900

The Sanctuary
in a New Muslim Order

The next eight hundred years of Jerusalem's history began with a century and a half of considerable turmoil fostered by the Crusades, and ended with several centuries of relative peace before the struggles of the twentieth century. The Dome of the Rock weathered it all without significant alterations in its appearance, except for a new external skin of colorful ceramic tiles acquired in the sixteenth century. The building did, however, undergo all sorts of minor renovations and repairs as well as a fascinating evolution in meaning, or meanings. Around 1400, it acquired the standard set of religious and pious associations that have remained more or less unaltered today. Throughout this period once again we encounter an unusual feature of this building: that changes in meaning were not significantly reflected in changes of form.

The Crusaders

Jerusalem was stormed by the Crusaders on July 15, 1099. The Muslim defenders of the city were defeated and much of the population was killed. The Haram, especially the Aqsa Mosque, was the scene of some of the most repellent massacres. The Dome of the Rock was looted of most of its precious objects made of expensive metal, probably including the silver hanging lamps and some of the silver wall plaques. But otherwise the buildings of the Muslim holy space were undamaged.

The problem for the victorious Christians from the West was how to use these buildings, and most particularly the Dome of the Rock, in their newly created Latin Kingdom of Jerusalem. Strange though it may be, the Latin Christians seem to have made no clear association between the spaces and monuments of the Haram and a sacred or any other kind of history. Unlike the Holy Sepulcher or the sanctuaries of Mount Zion and the Mount of Olives, the Haram had been very rarely mentioned in Christian accounts between 700 and 1100. When it appeared, it was identified as the area of Solomon's Temple and palace. What seems to have occurred in Christian writings prior to the Crusades was a fascinating "reincarnation" of the Haram's major buildings as semi-mythical monuments known through Bible stories alone. Thus, the Dome of the Rock was interpreted as the Holy of Holies and the Aqsa Mosque as the Temple of Solomon. What was meant by this distinction between the two is not at all clear.

Once the Crusader conquest was completed, the Dome of the Rock was named the Temple of the Lord (Templum Domini), and the Aqsa Mosque was labeled the Temple of Solomon (Templum Solomonis). Here again, the distinction seems moot in historical terms, since Herod's building was either unknown or unrecognized at this time, and the Temple of the Lord, which Christians associated with the Presentation of the Virgin and with events in the life of Jesus, should have been assumed to be the same place as the Temple of Solomon. The distinction was made, I suggest, as a result of a visual judgment, not a historical one. While everyone knew that the original Jewish Temple had been destroyed, its reappearance as an impressive work of art made sense to Christians in the twelfth century, whenever it might have been rebuilt and whoever was responsible for its rebirth. The geometrically perfect, centrally planned, beautifully decorated domed structure seemed appropriate for a direct relationship to the divine, and thus it became in their minds the Temple of the Lord. The spread-out and less clearly focused congregational mosque could be imagined as a royal dwelling, which conjured up the palace of Solomon, with its nearby temple.

William of Tyre, the main chronicler of the Crusades, born in Syria around 1130 and associated with the local ecclesiastical hierarchy, was better informed. He attributed the Dome of the Rock to the Muslim caliph 'Umar (hence the historically untenable appellation Mosque of Omar, which has stuck with the building ever since). Allegedly, the caliph wanted to reconstruct the Temple of the Lord (that is, the Lord Jesus Christ) that had been destroyed by the Romans. William of Tyre makes no mention of anything Jewish having to do with the Temple, but curiously he recognized the existence of mosaic inscriptions which he could not read but which, according to him, mentioned "who rebuilt the temple, when, and at what cost." He must have been referring to the Umayyad inscription in Arabic on the interior octagonal arcade.

Little by little, more specific Christian events became associated with the Dome of the Rock: Abraham's near-sacrifice of Isaac (Genesis 22:6–14); Jacob's stone pillow and his dream (Genesis 28:10–22); David's encounter with the angel and his purchase of a threshing-floor for the site of the Temple (2 Samuel 24:15–25); the stoning of Zachariah between the porch and the altar of the Temple (2 Chronicles 24: 20–22); the meeting of Joachim and Anna in the Temple and the Presentation of the Virgin (as told by an apocryphal text known as the *Protoevangelium of James*); the Presentation of Christ in the Temple and the prophecy of Simeon (Luke 2:22–40); the archangel Gabriel announcing to another Zachariah that he would have a son, John the Baptist (Luke 1:5–24); Jesus among the doctors (Luke 2:46–52); Jesus chasing the money-changers out of the Temple (Matthew 21:12–13); Jesus forgiving the adulterous woman (John 8:2–11); Peter and John healing a lame man at the Golden Gate (Acts 3:1–11). For a Western Christian public made up of priests, monks, and pious or adventurous men and women seeking the spaces of holy history, the Dome of the Rock became a convenient haven for many sacred events other than the ones formally connected with the ancient Temple of Jerusalem.

A selection of these associations was confirmed by a series of panels, probably constructed of wood, which were covered with writing and hung inside the Dome of the Rock. John of Würzburg, who wrote a long letter describing Jerusalem around 1170, lists most of these inscriptions, many of which are excerpts from appropriate prayers used in the liturgy. The Presentation of Jesus in the Temple included a particularly lengthy and didactic explanation. Also inside the building, two extensive inscriptions, removed after the Muslim reconquest, were set in the drum of the dome. The lower one mixes Isaiah 56:7 from the Old Testament with Matthew 7:7–8 and 21:13 from the New Testament. The upper one is exclusively from the Old Testament: 3 Kings 8–28 and Deuteronomy 26:15. These inscriptions did not replace the earlier Arabic ones, which, to a general public ignorant of the Arabic language, probably seemed to be mere ornament.

A more peculiar written addition was made on the outside of the building. At the top of the dome: "Eternal peace on this house be from God the Lord eternally; blessed be the glory of God from His holy place" (Ezekiel 3:2). Toward the south: "Well-founded is the house of the Lord on a firm rock. Blessed are they who dwell in the house of the Lord. From generation to generation they shall praise thee" (Psalm 84:5 and parts of the breviary). Toward the east: "Truly the Lord is in this place, and I did not know it. Lord in thy house all praise thy glory" (Genesis 28:16 and Psalm 29:9). Toward the north: "The Temple of the Lord is holy, God's labor and building" (Psalm 65:6).

All the inscriptions were set above the marble and mosaics of the Umayyad building, either as friezes of large letters below the parapet or as stone or bronze plaques hung on the wall. The Christian sponsors of these inscriptions may have been influenced by the Muslim use of writing as decoration and may have felt, consciously or not, that writing carried their message better than images. John of Würzburg, writing nearly three generations after the Christians' brutal conquest of the city and the massacre of its Muslim population, was aware of Muslim opinion in his time. He frequently notes the negative views of the "Saracens," or Muslims, toward changes made by Christians. They were enraged by the Cross fixed on top of the Dome of the Rock, and they were shocked by the image of Christ above the western entrance to the building. But the inscription above that door, also taken from the Scriptures and shared by the Old and New Testaments (Isaiah 56:7 and Matthew 21:13), is less partisan: "This house of Mine shall be called a house of prayer." Its tone has a universal appeal, recalling the seventh-century Muslim inscriptions which avoided references that would have been unacceptable to Christians.

As was so often the case when the Holy Land was reinterpreted in the Middle Ages, the existence of the Dome of the Rock preceded the explanation of its meaning, as though the building was waiting for new meanings to be assigned to it. A few Latin writers acknowledged that the Dome of the Rock was built by and for Muslims (or "pagans," as they were called), and some even believed that these "pagans" went there to worship an idol of the Prophet Muhammad. According to a poem of the time, the idol was a statue of silver covered with gold and jewels, so heavy that it required six strong men to carry it outside in order to be destroyed.

Christian writers often associated Muslims with the pagans of the Roman Empire—a group much better known in the collective memory of Western Christians—and assumed that Muslims shared those pagan practices. This is a wonderful instance, not un-known in our own times, of a psychological, perhaps even spiri-tual, process in which human history is subsumed within a rich baggage of legendary, mythical, or pious stories that bear no rela-tionship to the historical record. One result of the behavior and at-titude of the Crusaders was that Muslims themselves—banned from the sanctuary and at times from the entire city—forgot the relationship that had previously existed between events and spaces on the Haram.

In addition to changes in meaning, the Crusaders brought with them minor changes in forms. They attached paintings and in-scriptions, probably of wood or stone, to existing walls, columns, and piers. These did not provide the building with a new skin but more like a new set of clothes. Practical, technical changes were made as well. For example, the Rock was covered with a wood and marble platform, and an altar was set on the platform for the cele-bration of the liturgy. A beautiful grille of wrought iron was ar-ranged around the Rock and was largely preserved until the 1960s (Fig. 42), when it was removed to the Haram Museum, where it can be seen today. A number of small sculpted items from the Latin Christian period, such as capitals or entablatures, remain in the building, but their original purpose is no longer clear.

The modifications carried out by the Crusaders did not take place immediately after the conquest. The new secular and reli-gious masters of the city may have felt overwhelmed by their suc-cess and in need of time to understand what they had acquired and to figure out how to deal with its many features. They also had a

42. Iron grille erected by the Crusaders, now in the Haram Museum.
(Courtesy of the Fine Arts Library, Harvard College Library.)

more practical problem. In the period before a suitable palace
could be constructed in the area of the citadel of Jerusalem to the
west, the Haram served as royal quarters and as the place where
coronations and other ceremonies took place. Monks from the Au-
gustinian order settled just north of the Dome of the Rock as early
as 1112. This is probably when the Rock was covered with marble,
allegedly to protect it from vandals who broke off pieces of it to sell
as relics from the holy city. Services began to be celebrated there

right away, but the formal dedication of the Dome of the Rock as a Christian church did not take place until 1141. Probably Queen Melisende, widow of the second Latin king of Jerusalem and the sponsor of many works of art in the kingdom, ordered the grille placed around the Rock.

Circumstantial evidence suggests that the panels with inscriptions were hung after 1150. At some point, the cavern under the Rock came to be used as a confessional, and a handsomely decorated entrance with Romanesque columns is still there today to provide an internal direction in a building that had not emphasized direction before. Some scholars have proposed that Queen Melisende and possibly other dignitaries of the time hoped to be buried inside the Dome of the Rock. This would have continued the common Christian practice of burying notable persons within churches. And in a way it would have connected the Dome of the Rock and the Haram with the places to the east of the Haram that had for centuries been associated with death and resurrection and where Christians, Muslims, and Jews were buried.

With this possibility in mind, we can summarize the activities of the Crusaders in the following manner. They were very vague on the actual historical background of the building, but they asserted that it was the Temple of the Lord, that is to say, the Jewish Temple as it existed at the time of Christ. And this belief helped protect the building. Whatever the Christians did to it accentuated its features while preserving its decoration. In a sense, the Crusaders accepted the aesthetic power of the Muslim monument and simply adopted it as part of their own history. Even more significantly, they imitated its form when building a new memorial to the Ascension of Christ on top of the Mount of Olives, thus celebrating again one of the great sacred themes of the city of Jerusalem, the resurrection and the expectation of eternal life.

The Crusaders and their successors made far more explicit than did their Muslim predecessors the specific meanings they attached to the building, and they used the same media, primarily writing, to make these meanings visible. This transformation worked for Christians because the meaning of the building as developed by Muslims over the previous two centuries had not yet jelled into either a definitive formal expression or a cultural mandate. Within certain limits, the building's forms could have been interpreted differently by Christians, but they did not necessarily have to be: foot and hand imprints on rocks, a belief in divine judgment and resurrection, and pilgrimage to religious shrines were common to both religions. Overwhelmed by the aesthetic qualities of the monument, the Crusaders simply made meanings explicit in their own pious language without changing the building's form.

Meanwhile, the pious meanings that Muslims associated with the Dome of the Rock disappeared or withered away with the massacre or eviction of the Muslim population after 1099. This created an unusual sort of problem following the Muslim reconquest almost a century later, in 1187: to reconstruct or reinvent a Muslim past for this sacred space. We do possess the rare testimony of a Muslim visitor in 1173, al-Harawi, who recognized the Rock as the place where the Prophet ascended into heaven. He seems to have understood the cavern under the Rock as the place where the spirits of believers await resurrection. Al-Harawi saw and read, in part, a Fatimid inscription that had been left untouched, and while he noticed the presence of Christian images, he added that the Christians did not change much in the building. Curiously, while providing once again a list of measurements of every element of construction in the Dome of the Rock, al-Harawi did not describe the character of the building as a whole.

To close this relatively short episode in the history of the Dome of the Rock, I will mention another phenomenon for which the Crusaders were responsible, though it did not take place in Jerusalem but probably in northern Syria and the upper Mesopotamian Valley under the rule of local feudal lords like the Ayyubids (about whom I will have more to say shortly). Recent scholarship has associated with Jerusalem and the Dome of the Rock the fascinating practice by Muslim artisans of making silver-inlaid bronze objects with Christian scenes. These scenes are the very ones that Muslims and Christians could commemorate together: the Presentation of the Virgin in the Temple, the Nativity, the Flight to Egypt, and so on. Both Muslims and Christians may have acquired these decorated objects of practical use (basins, candlesticks), for they were created during a short-lived period in the first half of the thirteenth century when the two faiths shared a patronage of religious themes within an aristocratic secular context. None of these objects contain representations of the Dome of the Rock, but they are all richly ornamental, as though reflecting in silver and bronze the glitter and rich texture of the interior design of the building in Jerusalem.

The Ayyubid Search for the Past

In 1187, after the battle of the Horns of Hattin in north central Palestine, the Crusaders surrendered Jerusalem to the victorious Ayyubid sultan Saladin. The exact date of the surrender was October 2 in the Christian calendar, and in the Muslim calendar the 27th day of the month of Rajab—the day celebrating the Ascension of the Prophet Muhammad, whom the faithful in the larger Muslim community firmly associated with the Haram in Jerusalem. The city was briefly retaken by the complex and ambitious Holy Roman emperor Frederick II in 1229 but lost again to an Ayyubid ruler in 1244. The Haram itself, however, remained entirely in Muslim hands after 1187, and in 1250 Ayyubid rule by feudal lords was replaced by that of the Mamluks of Egypt. At that point Jerusalem became a provincial city within a larger political entity.

Yet the sixty odd years of Ayyubid rule were important, for two reasons. One is that the return of Jerusalem to Muslim hands was an event celebrated throughout the Islamic world, and the many accounts we have of the reconquest itself or of the first sermon pronounced on the Haram by the chief judge Muhi al-Din ibn al-Zaki testify to the pan-Islamic recognition of Jerusalem's rank among the holy places of Islam. The challenges were to define the nature of that holiness, to identify the Muslim character of all the sacred places taken over by Christians, and to label them with inscriptions and possibly other specific signs so as to avoid the loss of meaning that had occurred during occupation by the Crusaders.

The other reason for the importance of the short Ayyubid period is that the Muslim world itself had changed enormously during the twelfth century. A very different Islamic society had replaced the Abbasid and Fatimid cultures that characterized the eleventh century. Kurdish and Turkic military leaders predominated, and the forbidding citadel had replaced the palace or the governor's abode as the symbol of power. A Sunni revival had reduced the importance of Shi'ite movements and more or less incorporated much of mystical Sufism within its fold. Buildings with socially useful purposes—religious schools of all sorts, hospitals, *ribats* and other restricted dwellings for men, hostels and caravansaries, public fountains—were sponsored by a range of patrons and replaced the large mosques of the previous era. A mausoleum for the founding patron was often included in the composition of these monuments. Angular or floriated kufic writing gave way to the more fluid cursive known as *naskhi,* which tended to be provided with all diacritical marks and was therefore easier to read. Changes of similar importance occurred in the making of books and in the design of art objects. Altogether, a new Muslim society, more varied in its ethnic components and richer in its religious and social culture, appeared in Jerusalem after 1187.

How did all of this affect the Dome of the Rock? Christian images and inscriptions as well as the marble floor set over the Rock were removed, and the Rock itself was washed and perfumed. The surrounding grillework was preserved in part, but an Ayyubid wooden screen was added to enclose an area that had been accessible for Christian liturgies. Inscribed on that screen was the name of the patron, a son of Saladin, which dates it to 1199. The inscription also included the names of the woodworker, Abu al-Khayr ibn Abi Ali, and two designers, Abu Bakr and Uthman, both sons of a pilgrim to Mecca *(hajji)* simply named Musa, without mention of a patronymic or a place of origin. The recording of the names of artisans is a sign of a new recognition in the Ayyubid period of different social orders and possibly of the participation in the reconstruction of the city of new, spiritually inclined immigrants to Jerusalem.

A more important Ayyubid statement was made through a long inscription in gold mosaics on a green background at the base of the drum of the dome (a fragment is visible in Fig. 31). The inscription is in the newly developed cursive script and elegant in style. It contains occasional dots in mother-of-pearl over and under appropriate letters, just as the great Umayyad inscription of 691 did. Writing forms only the upper third of the mosaic band, whose lower two thirds display the relatively common motif of an arcade with dotted arches and, under the arch, medallions that are neither simply vegetal nor geometric but give the impression of a succession of wheels. The motif may be a transformation, with a vaguely architectural overlay, of the border that decorated the bronze plaques of the seventh century. The use of these older mosaic techniques makes it reasonable to date the whole ornamental band to the reign of Saladin, since several other mosaic inscriptions from his time exist in Jerusalem, especially in the Aqsa Mosque. The technique may have been revived because patrons associated it with the original structures on the Haram and with the power and authority of the past. Alternatively, the use of mosaics may have been simply a sign of ostentation and wealth.

This parallel with the original Umayyad decoration is further confirmed by the content of the inscription. Except for its beginning and end, it is entirely Qur'anic and contains verses 1 to 21 of surah 20, known as "Ta-Ha" from the two mysterious letters with which it begins. The full text of the inscription goes as follows: "In the name of God the Compassionate, the Merciful, *ta ha. We have not revealed unto thee [Muhammad] this Qur'an that thou should be distressed, but as a reminder unto him that fears, a revelation from Him who created the earth and the high heavens, the Beneficent one, who is established on the throne. To Him belongs whatsoever is in the heavens and whatsoever is in the earth, and whatsoever is between them, and whatsoever is beneath the soil. And if thou speakest aloud, then indeed He knows the secret* [thought] *and* [that which is yet] *more hidden. God! There is no God save Him. His are the most beautiful names.*

"*Has there come unto thee the story of Moses? When he saw a fire and said to his people: Wait indeed I see a fire far off. See how I may bring you a brand therefrom or may find guidance at the fire. And when he reached it, he was called by name: O Moses I indeed am thy lord. So take off thy shoes, for verily thou art in the holy valley of Tuwa* [thought to be near Mount Sinai]. *And I have chosen thee, so hearken unto that which is inspired. I indeed am God. There is no God but Me. So serve Me and perform prayer for My remembrance. The hour is indeed coming. But I will to keep it hidden, so that every soul may be rewarded for that which it strives to achieve. Therefore let not such as believe not therein but follow their own caprices divert thee therefrom, less thou perish. And what is this in thy right hand, O Moses? He said: This is my staff on which I lean and with which I bend down branches for my sheep and for which I find other uses. He said: Cast it down, O Moses! So he cast it down and behold it was a serpent, gliding. He said: Grasp it and fear not we shall return it to its former state.* God Almighty is right."

How should we interpret this striking passage from one of the most powerful surahs of the Holy Book, one which is usually read at funerals and which, according to legend, is most frequently uttered in Paradise? First of all, since the inscription contains no historical reference to a personage or a date, we can assume that its value was primarily meant to be spiritual and, one might almost say, iconographic in the sense that its content is more significant than its presence as a decorative border. Furthermore, these verses were otherwise never used on either buildings or objects. Their message is, therefore, specific to the holy city and to the Dome of the Rock.

One interpretation proposed by Miriam Rosen-Ayalon is that the inscription reflects the events of 1187 and the ideology surrounding the re-establishment of Muslim authority over the building. A sanctuary associated, even indirectly, with Moses had been transformed into an evil snake by the Christians and would now be restored to its ordained Muslim purpose. But the fact that the quotation contains more than this fragment of the story of Moses and that the rest of the surah elaborates on many of the themes mentioned in its first twenty verses allows me to propose a different explanation for its meaning in this particular context.

My explanation has two facets. One is in a sense personal, *ad hominem*. A peculiarity of the chosen passage and many that follow is that God is constantly conversing with Moses, as he did in the Bible, and organizes simultaneously Moses' own salvation and the salvation of his people, just as happened with Saladin who, with the help of God, returned Jerusalem to Islam and to God. It is therefore reasonable to see Saladin as a new Moses and to suggest a relationship between Moses and political leadership that will appear more than once in Islamic political mythology. One of its most original expressions in Palestine, in the hills overlooking the Jordan Valley, is a sanctuary to Moses built at the presumed site of his tomb. By the end of the thirteenth century this sanctuary would became a major symbol of Muslim possession of the Holy Land, even though the Bible is quite explicit in stating that Moses died before ever reaching the Promised Land.

But there is more. "The hour is coming," says the holy text; the resurrection and subsequent judgment are about to arrive, and many passages in the rest of the surah are full of references to death and eternal life: "From the earth did We create you and into it shall We return you and from there We shall bring you out again" (55); "and indeed I am forgiving toward him who repents and believes and does good, and afterward walks aright" (82). After constant references to "the day when the trumpet [of the Last Judgment] is blown" (102), the surah ends with a reminder of the many messages sent to foretell the coming of Islam, a theme close to the one of the Umayyad inscriptions of 691, and with a dramatic statement of hope for the just: "Each one is awaiting; so await ye! You will come to know who are the owners of the path of equity and who is right" (135). Like many visually transmitted messages in medieval Christian as well as Muslim iconography, this inscription does not contain the complete statement but operates through a fragment that implies the whole.

Recalling, then, the early connections made between the Rock and the original presence of God on earth as well as the preparation for His return, we may interpret Saladin's inscription as restating this grandiose vision of the building's significance and only indirectly proclaiming his own role in saving a holy place and bringing the faithful back to it. Nothing is said in this inscription, nor in any other one in the Dome of the Rock up to that time, about the Night Journey of the Prophet. What is proclaimed in a narrow and almost invisible band of writing is a far greater truth, the truth of divine presence and divine judgment.

Another and perhaps more mundane aspect of the Dome of the Rock in the Ayyubid period comes to light through an interesting practice developed at that time, the pilgrimage *(hajj)* by proxy. Wealthy or otherwise busy figures like Saladin sent someone else to accomplish the obligatory trip to Mecca for them, and they eventually received certification that their holy duties were completed; a number of these certificates (including Saladin's) are preserved in the Museum of Turkish and Islamic Art in Istanbul. Some of the documents were accompanied by painted paper rolls with simplified images of Mecca and Medina. A few represented the two layers of Jerusalem's prominent dome as being under construction (Fig. 43), or included a simple image of a foot on a rock (usually interpreted as Muhammad's) and a few other features of the sanctuary. In these images, curiously, elementary and simplified signs depicting commonly known items like minarets, mihrabs, or trees are displayed next to strongly emphasized unique fixtures like the Ka'bah in Mecca, the tomb of the Prophet in Medina, and the Dome of the Rock or the imprint of a foot in Jerusalem.

What is important for our outline of the evolution of the monument's significance is that in Ayyubid times Jerusalem and the Dome of the Rock finally entered fully into the triad of holy spaces for the Muslim faithful. Mecca, with its Ka'bah, was created through divine order and eventually became the direction of prayer for all believers. Medina, with its tomb, was the city where the Prophet was buried. Jerusalem, with the Dome of the Rock, was the first *qiblah* and the home of nearly all the prophetic forerunners of Muhammad, but even more important, at the end of time it would be the place of the resurrection and the gate to Paradise. These ideas and associations were not new in themselves, but for centuries pilgrimage to these three hallowed sites had not been available to the faithful because the Fatimids and other heretical movements had splintered the Muslim world into political entities at ideological loggerheads with one another. And then the Crusades further complicated access to the holy places. Only under the Ayyubids did the triad of Muslim sanctuary-cities come under one rule and become accessible to all pilgrims.

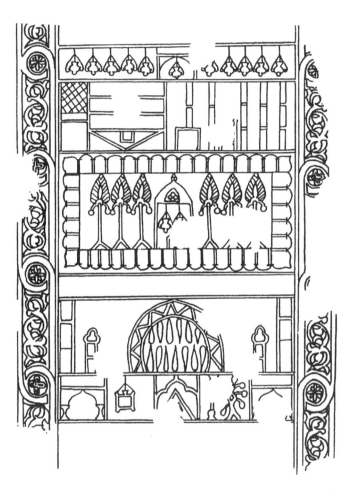

43. Sketch of the Dome of the Rock on a pilgrimage deed of the twelfth century in Istanbul. (After Milstein.)

This revival, this institutionalization, of old meanings gave originality to the Dome of the Rock in Ayyubid times. It was all made possible by the ideologies of Saladin's entourage, but also by a new governing mood. The political order was justified and run by a complex legal system and by several independent groups—the military, the legal and theological establishment, a revived school system, the merchants and artisans of the bazaar—committed to the preservation of that order. The following two and a half centuries were to witness its refinement.

The Shrine in a Mamluk Context

Mamluk rule over Jerusalem from the middle of the thirteenth century to 1516 was, for the most part, remarkably peaceful. The Christian danger was long gone, most Greek and Latin religious authorities had left, except for a handful of eastern Christian communities and the Franciscans, who held on to whatever they could. The Mongol onslaughts never reached Jerusalem, and no one bothered to repair the walls of a city so weakened by too many rulers. The center of power and authority was in Cairo, and the two Syrian cities of Damascus and Aleppo were major cultural and economic hubs often competing with the Egyptian metropolis. For a while even the population of Jerusalem declined.

Administratively and politically, Jerusalem was of secondary importance, but it came to play an interesting social role in the complicated hierarchy of power that ruled the Levant and Egypt. The city became the place where failed competitors to the rulers in

Egypt were sent in exile, usually with their assets intact, which they were supposed to spend on the holy city. The result was a fairly rapid repopulation and especially an extraordinary program of construction within the city. Schools, religious madrasahs, hospices, private houses, retirement homes, commercial fountains, and public cisterns were built in amazing numbers. Some sixty-four structures are still more or less preserved and have been catalogued in the admirable survey of Mamluk Jerusalem conducted by the British School of Archaeology in Jerusalem (Fig. 44).

These buildings were concentrated on the northern and western sides of the Haram and on the streets leading to it from the west (Figs. 45 and 46). The Mamluk administration gave the Old City of Jerusalem a unified look, and still today Jerusalem is the best preserved example anywhere in the world of a Mamluk city with the unique architecture of its time. These structures created for visitors and pilgrims a monumental access—a sort of honor guard leading up to the Haram—and an equally monumental setting, whose superb stone masonry and occasional doorways topped by half-domes on stalactites, often punctuated with inscriptions praising the generosity of donors and the power of their patrons, accompany the visitor and prepare him for the holy space of the sanctuaries, different from the worldly spaces of urban life. Viewed from the top of the Mount of Olives to the northeast, the Dome of the Rock sits on its platform as on a grand stage, with Mamluk architecture as its backdrop. This vision of the Haram was then the only one available to non-Muslims, and even today it has remained the favorite point of view for most drawings and photographs by Western travelers.

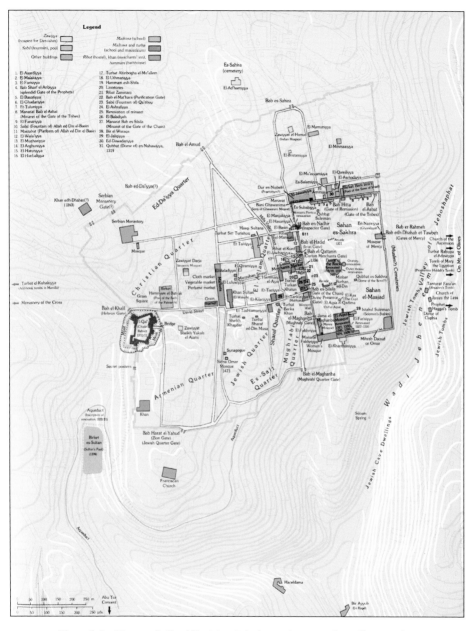

44. Plan of the Haram al-Sharif in Mamluk times. (From Bahat, *Illustrated Atlas of Jerusalem.*)

45. The northern side of the Haram al-Sharif, showing the facades of Mamluk religious schools. (Z. Radovan / BibleLandPictures.)

How aware the Mamluks were of the visual effect their many monuments would have on Jerusalem's image, near and far, is hard to know. Their investment in the city was mostly restricted to a small number of places that had been heavily built up by the Crusaders. The area needed to be given a Muslim character, and its ruined buildings provided raw materials for construction. But the

46. The western side of the Haram al-Sharif, with a fifteenth-century fountain and a Mamluk colonnade.

Mamluks were conscious of the value of urban planning and the symbolic dimension of architecture. To them, the recovery of Jerusalem and the defeat of the Crusaders was a major event celebrated by the transfer of whole Gothic gateways to Cairo and the representation of the Dome of the Rock on the facade of the grandiose madrasah of Sultan Hassan (see Fig. 20). Two small mosques on either side of the Holy Sepulcher in Jerusalem were provided with tall minarets to proclaim Islam's victory over the most sacred church in all of Christendom.

During this momentous transformation of the city, very little about the Dome of the Rock itself was changed. The outside mosaic decoration, whose details are practically unknown, was restored under the rule of Baybars (1260–1277). Muhammad ibn Qala'un (1299–1309) had the dome gilded anew. Probably under al-Nasir Muhammad, around 1327–1328, the ceiling of the outer ambulatory was redone in gilded and painted plaster with intricate floral and geometric designs; this ceiling was faithfully restored in 1960–1961. In 1447 part of the dome was hit by lightning (or, in an alternative version, damaged by a child chasing pigeons in the rafters) and its whole western side was destroyed and restored. Except perhaps for the ceiling of the outer ambulatory, these activities did not significantly affect the appearance of the building.

A more unusual innovation was the introduction of a marble rostrum into the southern part of the building, near the entrance to the cave under the Rock. It was neatly fitted between two columns of the circular arcade and set on ten meager columns whose capitals were reused from a Crusader construction. Now removed to the Haram Museum, the rostrum is a restoration, completed in 1387, of something earlier. The accompanying inscription calls it a *sudda*, a high bench that could be a pulpit for a preacher or a stand for reciters of the Qur'an, who frequently held endowed positions in late medieval sanctuaries. Mujir al-Din, the Mamluk chronicler of Jerusalem, refers to this structure as a *dikka al-mu'adhdhinin*, a "platform for the muezzins" who call the faithful to prayer. But the Dome of the Rock was not a mosque, and there was no minaret nearby. It is possible, but not very likely, that the muezzins gathered for prayer in the Dome of the Rock before marching to the minarets on the western edges of the Haram and then calling the whole city to prayer. A later inscription (1582) refers to the enlargement of the rostrum and calls it a *mahfil*, "gathering place," a word that in Ottoman times designated the place of the ruler in the mosque.

Altogether, the function or functions of this addition to the Dome of the Rock seems to have been a source of some confusion. Since its shape puts it within the category of the furniture normally associated with a congregational mosque, its presence may be connected with the inclusion, probably in Mamluk times, of a mihrab indicating the direction of prayer and of a *minbar* or pulpit for a preacher, all standard requirements for a place of prayer. But the building itself could not easily accommodate a congregation. If we consider the appearance on the Haram itself of several small platforms with mihrabs, as well as a fancy stone pulpit restored in 1388 by Burhan al-Din, a local judge, we may conclude that the entire Haram had become a gathering place where different social or religious groups performed ritual obligations as separate entities on a vast common sacred space. The Dome of the Rock could have been reserved for one of these groups, or, more likely, it could have served as a symbolic or practical center for all Muslims. One of its functions was the public reading of the Qur'an, a continuous task carried out by a staff of professional readers in a manner that has parallels in Christian and Buddhist sanctuaries.

In short, we can detect something practical, not to say prosaic, about the Dome of the Rock in Mamluk times. The sources from this period say very little about the original reasons for its construction. Both Ibn Battutah, the great Moroccan traveler of the fourteenth century, and Mujir al-Din report that the Prophet ascended into heaven from the Rock, but the matter is mentioned without particular emphasis and without details that had already been developed as early as the eleventh century. At least so it seems from looking at texts written by standard Sunni authorities from the Arabic-speaking world. But if we go further afield, we find that the story of the Ascension of the Prophet became a major theme of religious literature in Iran and in Central Asia in the fourteenth century, coinciding more or less with the time of Dante's visionary poem of other worlds. Even Persian miniatures of this time illustrate various aspects of the Prophet's mystical journey, one of which represents a totally fictitious Jerusalem (see Fig. 16). When the pious associations of the Dome of the Rock entered into the wider Muslim world, the monument lost its original form and merged with a Jerusalem of fantasy—an imaginary city still cultivated today in the popular Islam of India and Indonesia (Fig. 47).

47. Dome of the Rock in an Indian popular postcard, featuring a total transformation of the space in which the Dome is located for a more powerful presentation of the shrine.

Probably at this time a curious new wrinkle in the interpretation of the Rock itself developed, more so in popular observance than in learned levels of Islamic theology. In his description, Mujir al-Din cites an earlier source attributed to the eleventh-century theologian Abu Bakr Ibn al-Arabi that is a commentary on Qur'an 23:18: "We [God] sent water down from heaven in a measured way and We caused it to soak in the soil and We certainly are able to drain it off." Ibn al-Arabi explains that all the waters of the earth come from under the Rock in Jerusalem. The Rock is unique, he says, in that it is not bound to anything on earth and is held miraculously from above. It does have the trace of the Prophet's foot on the south side, and it leans toward the south through fear of or respect for the Prophet. On the other side are traces of the fingers of angels who held it while it bent under the weight of Muhammad. (These are explained today as the Prophet's fingers holding down a Rock that wanted to fly away with him.)

Mujir al-Din quotes Ibn al-Arabi as saying that he became terrified at the idea of going underneath the Rock. But "when I saw wicked people who had practiced all sorts of sins enter and then come back safely, I decided to go in. Yet, I said to myself, maybe they had obtained an extension [to make up for their sins], but I will be punished immediately. This thought made me hesitate some more. But then I entered and saw myself surrounded by extraordinary miracles. One sees in fact the Rock entirely separated from the earth to which nothing ties it. And in some places it is farther [from the earth] than in others." Mujir al-Din then comments that everyone still knows that the Rock was formerly suspended between heaven and earth. This was so until a pregnant woman went down under it and became so frightened to be in such a space that she had a miscarriage. Then a wall was built connecting the Rock to the earth. And Mujir al-Din adds that it had to have been done after Ibn al-Arabi's visit in 1091–1092, although he does not provide a specific time.

Why did such a story develop in Mamluk times? It is related to constant themes of Jerusalem, and more specifically of the Dome of the Rock, like the Creation, the eventual Redemption associated with the site, and the Ascension of the Prophet. The story continues, in a new key, the dialogue between a peculiar space and divine revelation. It incorporates an existing structure and long-standing beliefs with basic human fears of death and the unknown. It invents a scientifically implausible phenomenon, the suspended rock, and then introduces a prosaically physical event, a miscarriage, to explain a major change in the space.

What is particularly remarkable about the story for our purpose is that it totally ignores the building, except to praise perfunctorily its shape and decoration. Useful things like liturgical prayers and the reading of the scriptures took place there, but they did not figure prominently in representations of the space by those who wrote about it in the Mamluk period.

The Ottoman Empire

In 1516 the Ottoman sultan Selim the Grim occupied Jerusalem as part of his systematic incorporation of the Mamluk realm into the Ottoman Empire. The city was now run by administrators appointed by the sultan but who remained under the authority of the governors of Damascus in Syria or Sidon (a coastal city in what is now Lebanon). Jerusalem's special status as the third holy place in Islam was complicated by the presence in the city, especially from the seventeenth century onward, of significant Jewish and Christian communities with strong ties to their coreligionists in Europe. Finally, in ways that are only beginning to be uncovered, a strong local aristocracy developed in Jerusalem around this time, whose names are still prominent among Palestinian notables. Power as well as patronage was shared between alien Ottoman appointees and local families. Thus a very different structure of patronage from the Mamluk one took control of Jerusalem—a structure that left an enormous amount of legal and administrative documentation as well as personal recollections by local leaders, only a few of which have been published.

The Ottomans preserved the Mamluk city, at least in the area of the Haram, but modified considerably the Haram itself and changed the outer skin of the Dome of the Rock in a spectacular way. On the Haram, the main alteration was the multiplication of cupolas or little platforms with mihrabs, especially on the upper platform. This implies a considerable diversification in the groups that used the Haram for all sorts of activities, in addition to prayer. A local notable, Abu al-Fath al-Dajani, who died in 1660, complained about the alluring perfumes used by praying women and about the rowdiness of the crowd after hearing a sermon preached from the roof of the Dome of the Rock. During one of the feasts, he relates, all the monuments were lit up for no reason at all, and revelries followed prayer—a non-Islamic foreign custom, according to him. It is a sin, he wrote, not to complain about such behavior, and one must rise against such practices.

These may have been the reactions of a local sourpuss, but even if we allow for some exaggeration, they conjure up a lively space in

which many different groups were involved in an array of social as
well as pious activities. A comparable phenomenon, on a much reduced scale, obtained among Jews and especially among Christians. The latter in particular used the streets of the city for their
processions, at least in later Ottoman times. These festivities were
not a daily occurrence, of course, but were connected to religious
feasts, such as the Muslim pilgrimage or fast and the Christian
Easter. The development and chronology of these practices are still
too little studied to allow for generalization, and the best information we have in hand comes from the nineteenth century.

The shape of Jerusalem was also affected by the activities of
Suleyman the Magnificent—called in Ottoman terms the Law-
Giver *(qanuni)*—who ruled from 1520 to 1566 and was the great or-
ganizer of the Ottoman realm. He was perfectly aware—as was the
ruling elite around him—of bearing the name of the great king
who built the Temple in Jerusalem, as well as the legendary palace
for the arrival of the Queen of Sheba. Furthermore, Suleyman felt
it essential for his prestige and authority to be seen as an active
Muslim ruler. One of the ways he expressed this ideological ambition was to proclaim himself the protector of the holy places, to
guarantee the safety of pilgrims, and to sponsor highly visible
transformations in the holy cities. In Jerusalem this meant first of
all the restoration of the city's walls, not so much to ward off unlikely attacks by Western Christians (although calls for Crusades
to reconquer Jerusalem did not disappear until the seventeenth
century) as to make strikingly visible the protective power of the
Ottoman ruler. These walls are still standing today, and even the

growth of a large city around them has not diminished their visual effect.

Suleyman's second major project was the restoration of the Dome of the Rock. Neither the archaeological record of the building nor the numerous written sources that deal with these repairs indicate whether these restorations were needed because of deterioration in the building or whether they were an expression of ideological piety. Both reasons were probably involved.

The main feature of Suleyman's work in the Dome of the Rock was the tile revetment of most of the outside of the building—the upper two thirds of the octagon and the drum. Altogether some 45,000 tiles were used, few of which are still in place today. Over the centuries, this decoration was much affected by the elements, and tiles were constantly replaced or reset without careful attention to their original position. In 1960–1962 the tiles were removed and new ones ordered that reproduced the original sixteenth-century design. How successful this effort was will not be known until studies of the fragments of the original decoration (most of which are kept in the Haram Museum) are published. We will then catch a glimpse of the operation, on a grand scale, of the industrial technology of tile making, one of the glories of classical Ottoman art. In the meantime, the present colorful surface of the building is beautiful in its own right, whether or not it faithfully copies the sixteenth-century design (Fig. 48).

A similar difficulty concerns the fifty-two windows in the octagon and the drum (Fig. 49). In Suleyman's time, all of them were redone with a stucco grid filled with stained glass. Like the tiles,

48. Detail of Ottoman tile work on exterior of Dome of the Rock, as redone in the twentieth century. (Jon Arnold Images / Alamy.)

these windows were often repaired over the centuries, and all of them were replaced by modern copies during restorations in the 1960s; the original windows are kept in the Haram Museum. The windows have been studied and published in two thick volumes on Ottoman Jerusalem sponsored by the British School of Archaeol-

49. Ottoman window and inscriptions on the outside.
(Jon Arnold Images / Alamy.)

ogy in Jerusalem. Suleyman's restorations, which can be dated to 1545–1551, perhaps even as late as 1561–1562, provide us with two interesting sets of information. One concerns their visual impact and associated meanings, and the other one involves their verbal statements, since writing predominates in the decoration of the windows.

The designs on the exterior walls consist mostly of the standard geometric and vegetal compositions found in much of Ottoman art. So far, it has not been possible to identify a pattern or rhythm in these designs to which one could attribute some iconographic significance. The simplest analysis, at this stage of our knowledge, considers each face of the octagon as bearing seven decorative panels and forming a succession of comparable pictures separated from one another by vertical panels and held together by a heavy entablature of writing. Further research may provide a more refined explanation for an effect that may too easily be dismissed as simply ornamental, but at a minimum we can say that Suleyman's teams of architects and craft masters maintained and strengthened the effect of light through color that had been part of the Dome of the Rock since Umayyad times. However, the flat hues of tile designs provide a different effect from a multiplicity of mosaic squares. The tiles were probably colder, more static, and less shiny, but far more spectacular when seen from afar, standing out as they did from the muted masonry of the urban skyline. Their main message was addressed to pilgrims and travelers, indicating the presence of a unique jewel of light amid barren hills and structures of stone.

This message was in striking contrast to that of Mecca, where in a deep valley a single cube covered with an ornamented black cloth did not so much dominate its surroundings as serve to draw in visitors; it was the *qiblah* toward which every Muslim strives. In Medina, the tomb of the Prophet dominated the much restored first mosque of Islam, but in a less dramatic setting than Jerusalem. This contrast among the three holy cities was reflected in the images and texts of later Ottoman religious manuals and souvenir books from the pilgrimage. In the cases of Mecca and Jerusalem, the visual structure of the cities reflected the presence in both places of symbols for the beginning of time (in Mecca, a house built by Adam or Abraham; in Jerusalem, traces of the Creator's foot) and for the end of time (the resurrection and last judgment in Jerusalem, the place for the trumpet of Isra'fil announcing the end of time in Mecca). The message that shines forth from Jerusalem is the promise of divine judgment and eternal life for the just (Fig. 50).

Such an interpretation, however tentative it may be, is partly confirmed by the written message on the exterior of the building. On the drum, just under the dome, is a large band dated 1545–1546 that contains verses 1 to 20 (truncated at the end) of surah 17, "The Children of Israel." It begins with the celebrated verse recalling the *masjid al-aqsa,* "the farthest mosque" to which God brought Muhammad by night. Then the surah recalls the message given to Moses and the admonition to follow its commands in order to avoid eternal punishment. It then proceeds to one of Muslim scripture's most striking statements about divine power, man's freedom of

50. Dome of the Rock as it appears in an Ottoman miniature of the seventeenth century. (Jerusalem, National and University Library, Yah. Ms. Ar. 117.)

action, and the ultimate divine judgment for which man needs to remain humble. Its last three verses are a moving exhortation: *"They fall down on their faces in tears and it increases their humility. Say: call upon God or call Rahman; by whatever name you call, for to Him belong the most beautiful names. Neither speak thy prayer aloud, nor speak it in a low tone, but seek a middle course. Say: praise be to God, who begets no son, and has no partner in His dominion; nor does He need any to protect Him from humiliation; indeed magnify Him for His greatness and glory."*

On the upper part of the octagon, the long band of inscriptions was redone in 1875 and once again in the middle of the twentieth century, but its topic is from the time of Suleyman. It consists of the whole of surah 36, the so-called "Ya-Sin" surah, which is one of the clearest expositions of the powers of God, the obligations of man, and the ultimate return of all things and people to God. It ends with the following words: *"Is not He who created the heavens and the earth able to create similar things? Indeed He is the supreme creator of knowledge. When He intends a thing, His command is 'Be' and it is. So glory to Him in whose hands is the dominion of all things; and to Him will you all be brought back."* This surah was often used on architectural monuments, and it is frequently recited at the time of death or at funerals.

Finally, the windows of the octagon contain inscriptions that include standard praises: the Throne Verse (2:255) proclaiming the absoluteness of divine power; parts of verse 9:18, which defines the character of those who visit sanctuaries; and the first five verses of surah 48, the surah of victory thanks to God's help. These quotations are all conventional fare in sacred Muslim buildings of the sixteenth century and earlier. What is important is that they are separated from one another by proclamations of the power of Suleyman, "Our lord, the sultan, the great king and honored *khaqan* [traditional Turkic title], lord of the necks of nations, sultan over Arabs and others."

These inscriptions can be seen as a sort of structure, comparable in a way to the hierarchical sequence of decoration inside an eastern Christian church. In the lowest part we find the requirements of the faith and the identification of the ruling monarch who sponsored the work. Above it is the proclamation of God's unique power over all creation. And finally, just under the dome lies a powerful statement of man's need for faith to meet divine judgment. All these ideas existed long before Ottoman times and were often associated with the Dome of the Rock in its earlier phases, but here they appear—as befits the time of Suleyman the Law-Giver—as the constituents of an organized religious order reconsecrating an old sanctuary for broad pious purposes, not just for the commemoration of discrete events or figures of old.

This inclusion of the Dome of the Rock in the imperial order of the Ottoman sultan was made clear by the rather grandiloquent inscription set on the tympanum of the northern entrance to the building (it was removed and is now kept in the Haram Museum). It says that this "cupola of God over the Rock *[qubbah Allah min al-sakhrah]* in His holy house *[baytihi al-muqaddas]*" was restored by Sultan Suleyman, all of whose claims to glory are then listed. It was a building, says the inscription, whose construction and brilliance are greater than all things, and Suleyman brought back its "ancient splendor *[al-baha' al-qadim]*" thanks to his talented architects. In short, Suleyman put a new robe on the Dome of the Rock, in the way that traditional Muslim rulers gave robes to their guests and subordinates. This robe proclaimed the power and the orderly principles of Ottoman rule.

Inside the building, much was repaired and redone, in particular the sequence of marble panels in the lower part of the wall and the ceilings in the ambulatories, probably also the mosaics. Major restoration campaigns are recorded for 1720–1721, 1742, 1754, 1780, 1817–1818, 1853, and 1874–1875, and the signatures of many artisans have remained. These documents are of much interest for the economic and technological history of the Ottoman Empire as well as Jerusalem. Their significance for the appearance of the building or the functions it fulfilled is more difficult to assess. But the Ottomans also made sure that the whole succession of repairs and restorations going back to Saladin would never be forgotten. They recorded them in summary form in long inscriptions in cartouches at the base of the dome, where copies of older inscriptions were constantly shortened to make room for new ones. Today's brilliantly lit dome is a fairly faithful rendition of the grandiose ornamental designs of the Ottoman tradition.

While not much was changed in appearance—color still dominated, and its basic form was hardly altered—the functions of the Dome of the Rock were modified in two ways under the Ottomans. One, befitting the order the empire fostered among people under its domination, was that prayer became the primary collective activity of the faithful—prayer performed in groups belonging to the same sectarian allegiances. Thus, special sections of the Haram were allotted to separate groups, whose leaders gathered first near or in the Dome of the Rock to prepare for the call to prayer and then moved to their assigned place on the esplanade. In this scheme, the Dome of the Rock was simply a sort of liturgical stepping stone, a particularly brilliant one, within a broader collective activity. The association of the Rock with the Ascension of the Prophet was recognized but does not seem to have played a significant role in descriptions or praises of the building and is only incidentally mentioned in inscriptions.

How, then, did the Ottomans account for the holiness of the Dome of the Rock? An extraordinary text by Abd al-Ghani al-Nabulusi (1641–1731) describes his visit to Jerusalem with a group of friends and followers from his hometown of Damascus and provides us with the beliefs of a learned Sunni scholar without connection to the Ottoman order. He attributes the building of the Dome of the Rock to the Crusaders—the Franks, as he calls them—who wanted to conceal through a building the fact that the Rock was separated from the soil around it and floated miraculously in midair. This incongruous idea, which first appeared in Mamluk times, was then illustrated in a number of popular Ottoman books showing an octagonal rather than square platform and a domed building with a suspended rock inside. To al-Nabulusi, the original purpose of the building was not to preserve or emphasize a presence or a memory but to conceal it, which is what the Crusaders sought to do. For al-Nabulusi, the suspended Rock became a mystical path toward truth, but a path that needed the beauty of the Dome of the Rock to attract the believer. And he composed poetry to illustrate his point:

> O God's Rock, the highly revered
> Whose love the heart of your passionate lover never gives up
> A spirit taking form in the depths of my thoughts,
> A light being embodied in what is visible to my eyes.
> A mole on the cheek of the sublime mosque
> A point from which all lines are determined
> . . .
> The truth has appeared through her concealments
> With an intimacy after long estrangement. . .
> She restricts her beauties for the eyes of her passionate lovers
> So her spectator always longs for her own spectacle

Was al-Nabulusi an exception, or does he illustrate a popular, as opposed to a learned and official, trend within traditional Islam—a trend that in the past had given rise to the stories surrounding the Ascension and that now took a different direction, focused on the past of the place itself rather than on the people or events that interacted with it? Further investigations in manuscript collections are needed to answer this question properly.

In the meantime, we can conclude that the Dome of the Rock operated in three ways during Ottoman times. First, it was an old sanctuary embedded within a newly organized statement of Islamic faith and practice. This sanctuary was a place of prayer for all Muslim believers, at least for all Sunnis, and the third holy place of the faith, described and illustrated in manuals and visited by pilgrims on a path that led ultimately to Medina and Mecca. Still the site of the first *qiblah,* it was, perhaps more important, the place of the forthcoming resurrection. A second meaning of the Dome of the Rock was as an esoteric, strange, and original place, built, in at least one story, by Christians to conceal an extraordinary example of divine power. This mystery and its attempted concealment were transformed by some into a subject of praise and meditation. And finally, in Iran, Central Asia, India, and elsewhere, Jerusalem and the Haram became places where the Prophet's mystical Night Journey was commemorated. Jerusalem itself was transformed into a fantasy, and its reality disappeared from view.

After about 1875, the Dome of the Rock remained as it had been under the Ottomans until the 1960s. Despite occasional repairs, for the most part it was left to age with time. Its dome became gray, and its decoration lost its luster because of accumulated soot and dirt. In the first half of the twentieth century it was not used much except by occasional pilgrims and elderly Muslims of Jerusalem; its interior became somber and shoddy. The massive renovations of 1959–1962 and then of the late 1990s restored something of the brilliance it had lost. This was accomplished through careful study of everything that remained from the past and through the use of the best available technology. We will never know whether the Ottoman or the Mamluk or the Fatimid or the Umayyad buildings were exactly like the present one. But, except perhaps for the arrangement of interior lights, the present Dome of the Rock is a reasonable approximation of what it was like in the last version we know of it. In recent times, the building has became crowded again and more frequently used than before. This has happened for political as well as social or religious reasons, as the old Umayyad sanctuary became a symbol of a new Palestinian nationalism.

Conclusion

The history of the Dome of the Rock from the moment of its foundation in 691 until today has one striking characteristic. Repaired and restored though its basic form has been over the centuries, it has hardly changed; only the surfaces have been adapted to new uses. The present gold-colored dome, constructed of a modern aluminum alloy, replaced a dull gray wooden dome covered with lead sheets that had, in turn, replaced a more colorful bronze cover. In the sixteenth century, mosaics on the exterior, about which we know little except for the obvious presence of color, were removed, and ceramic tiles were installed in their place. The modern system of interior lighting emphasizes the central cylinder and its dome, while its predecessor consisted of many hanging lamps that distributed light all over the building (though their actual effect is difficult to reconstruct without experimenting on the building or creating computer-generated models). Except perhaps for the lights, the visual impact of these different restoration techniques remained more or less the same throughout the centuries, and we can assume that future transformations will merely reflect new technologies and perhaps some minor modifications of taste, but they will not alter significantly a structure created over 1300 years ago.

While its forms have remained constant, the meanings associated with the Dome of the Rock have changed considerably, as have the functions it was expected to fulfill. Several different interpretations and uses may even have coexisted at times. From the very beginning, the building's basic purpose was commemoration within the Haram al-Sharif, a restricted Muslim compound of unusually large dimension. In that sense the Dome of the Rock belongs to a type of architecture found in the Muslim tradition in which the visual presence of the monument is far more important than the actions performed inside. This is why the Dome of the Rock could so easily become an icon of twentieth-century Israeli tourism and, simultaneously, a symbol of Palestinian nationalism. These meanings do not require presence in the building, only an image of it. And neither one of these contemporary appropriations would have been meaningful as recently as half a century ago.

Among the complicated mix of associations—sometimes contradictory or incompatible—that developed around the Dome of the Rock was, first, the extraordinary and unique commemoration of God's presence on earth and the preparation for His return to judge men and women at the end of time. The building was also the site of the Night Journey of the Prophet and his Ascension into heaven, as well as the first *qiblah* or direction of prayer for Muslims. Statements about the power and ambitions of Umayyad,

Abbasid, and Fatimid caliphs and of Ayyubid, Mamluk, and Ottoman sultans, along with memories of Hebrew prophets and heroes, were inscribed on its surface. For a few decades after the Crusades, even an assortment of Christian associations were made with the building. Though they did not survive locally, these Christian connections found an echo in the appearance of the Dome of the Rock in paintings by Raphael and Perugino and in the mysteries associated in popular myth with the Knights Templar (Fig. 51). One unusual link to Christianity was the belief, originating in Mamluk times, that the Dome was built by the Crusaders to conceal a Rock miraculously suspended in midair.

How were these various meanings possible in a form that changed so little? One explanation—derived from a general theory of architecture or even of art in its broadest sense—is that, like letters and syllables, architectural and perhaps ornamental forms do not necessarily have fixed meanings; they evolve as the context of their use changes. Only representations have more or less fixed meanings, and this is why they are so frequently destroyed, as were the images introduced into the building by the Crusaders. When architectural and ornamental forms are preserved, it is, in part, because the aesthetic values embodied in these works of art, being nonrepresentational, enhance whatever meanings society or political leadership attributes to them. In this sense, the Dome of the Rock belongs to a unique series of monuments in the history of art that includes the Pantheon in Rome, the Alhambra in Granada, the Great Mosque of Cordoba, the Hagia Sophia in Istanbul, and the Taj Mahal. All of these monuments survived conquests and major

changes in the surrounding culture and yet continued to flourish with their new associations.

Of course, these buildings survived for many reasons, but one of them was undoubtedly their sheer beauty. In our times of easy destruction, I find something soothing in being able to conclude that aesthetic values alone may move people to give the preservation of works of art primacy over cultural or even religious programs. Through its circular composition and its play with light and shadow, the Dome of the Rock belongs to a fascinating series of beautiful buildings which, from Santa Constanza in fourth-century Rome (Fig. 52) to the domes of Cairo, Isfahan, Sinan, and Sir Christopher Wren and eventually to the Guggenheim Museum in New York, focused on drumlike, circumambulatory forms, often with colorful surfaces in thousands of variations.

But this aesthetic judgment is not sufficient to explain the wealth of associations that accrued to the Dome of the Rock over twelve centuries of Islamic rule. A further reason can be found in the rich texture of Islamic culture during these centuries. It could be orderly and legalistic, mystical and imaginative, collectively or individually expressed, reflective of the surrounding world or rejecting of it. All these facets had their own history, but they could also operate simultaneously. Thus, the Dome of the Rock could be a single, traditional place for collective or individual prayer, a place for

51. *The Marriage of the Virgin* by Raphael, one of several Italian paintings in which the Dome of the Rock served as a model for the temple in the background. (Pinacoteca di Brera, Milan, Italy; Scala / Art Resource, NY.)

52. Santa Constanza in Rome, one of the early models for the Dome of the Rock. (Piranesi, *Interior of S. Costanza,* Gift of Belinda L. Randall from the collection of John Witt Randall, Fogg Art Museum; Katya Kallsen / Harvard University Art Museums.)

the commemoration of many early histories, and a hope for future salvation. In a manner with many parallels in Islamic art, visually powerful forms that were iconographically weak allowed a wide range of meanings. Within Islamic culture, the Dome of the Rock harbored all the needs and thoughts of Muslims, without requiring anything except the desire to follow the dictates of the faith.

As such, the building illustrates one of the noblest streaks of traditional Islam, its openness to mankind's individual aspirations within the boundaries outlined by the Revelation. And in this sense the building also reflects the city where it was built—a holy city, in so many different ways, for all three of the Semitic revealed religions. The Dome of the Rock sent a message of earthly power through its shining domination of Jerusalem's landscape, but it was also a message of eternal hope for the future of the just.

And this point leads to the dilemma facing us in the twenty-first century—how to think about the Dome of the Rock in the world today. I would like to mention four possibilities, each implying different procedures for mundane matters such as maintenance, for broader issues like visitor accessibility, and for emotional concerns like piety and ethnic or national allegiance.

First, the building can be thought of as a political symbol of an Islam-dominated but not exclusively Muslim Palestine. And as such it can be transformed into a place for legitimating power, as probably happened at the time of the Umayyad rulers of the seventh century and of the Frankish kings during the Crusades. Second, the building can be considered a restricted Muslim holy place, occasionally open to non-Muslim visitors but freely accessible to all the Islamic faithful, from Senegal to the Philippines, and meeting a variety of needs in these immensely varied communities. Third, the Dome of the Rock can be considered a work of world art, to be visited by millions of travelers who are unaware, for the most part, of the religious and political impulses that created the building and still surround it today. These tourists will respond to the brilliant visual qualities of the monument, both inside and out, rather than its religious or nationalistic program. And finally, this monument can be considered the temporary occupant of a Jewish holy space, the Temple Mount—the site of the destroyed Temple of Jerusalem, which, according to Jewish religious law, cannot be rebuilt until the coming of the Messiah but must be kept ready for that event. In this interpretation, the Dome of the Rock is a building standing in a sort of historical limbo.

Each one of these approaches entails different legal, financial, administrative, and consultative structures to operate successfully. None is working at the moment. The Haram is run through a complicated and unwritten compromise among several authorities, and if this situation is not addressed and corrected, the building is bound to suffer sooner or later. But then, however moving the Dome of the Rock may be as a religious sanctuary or a work of art, it was never expected to impart wisdom. Wisdom, unfortunately, can come only from men and women, and over recent decades they have not shown much of it.

Bibliography

Index

Bibliography

The purpose of this essay is not to provide a complete bibliographical introduction to the subject. It is rather to identify the original sources I have used as well as the scholarly works from which I have benefitted and then to sketch out directions for further research by recognizing those sources and studies that are particularly important for the continuing pursuit of understanding an extraordinary building in a most remarkable city. It is almost impossible to separate the bibliography on the Dome of the Rock from the immense literature on Jerusalem since the Muslim take over in the seventh century, and the first section of this essay includes general books dealing with Jerusalem in the Middle Ages. Some of these have several authors and their chapters vary enormously in quality and usefulness. But all of them contain information, pictures, or ideas that are not found elsewhere. And most of them have long and elaborate bibliographies of their own. Then I turn to the Dome of the Rock itself at the time of its creation in 691, followed by the main sources for its history divided into five sections: 700 to 1100, the Crusades, Ayyubids, Mamluks, and Ottomans.

General Works

Bahat, Dan. *The Illustrated Atlas of Jerusalem.* Jerusalem, 1990. Clear drawings.

Ben-Dov, Meir. *Historical Atlas of Jerusalem.* New York, 2002. A populist work with revealing but not always reliable drawings.

Elad, Amikam. *Medieval Jerusalem and Islamic Worship.* Leiden, 1995. An imaginative and intelligent use of the *fada'il* literature.

Gil, Moshe. *A History of Palestine, 634–1099.* In Hebrew, Tel Aviv, 1983; in English, Cambridge, 1992. An excellent survey of sources and an old-fashioned historical account.

Gonen, Rivka. *Contested Holiness: Jewish, Muslim, and Christian Perspectives on the Temple Mount in Jerusalem.* Jersey City, 2003. Balanced survey with emphasis on the contemporary scene.

Grabar, Oleg. *The Shape of the Holy.* Princeton, 1996. An attempt to reconstruct the Muslim spaces of early Islamic times.

Hoyland, Robert G. *Seeing Islam as Others Saw It.* Princeton, 1997. A very rich array of documents and commentaries on the early Islamic period.

Ibrahim, Mahmud. *Fada'il Bayt al-Muqaddas.* Kuwait, 1985. An incomplete but useful selection of sources.

Kaplony, Andreas. *The Haram in Jerusalem 324–1099.* Stuttgart, 2002. A ground-breaking book in which visual materials, texts, inscriptions, and secondary materials are presented as they define a carefully described space. Difficult to use.

Livne-Kafri, Ofer. *Jerusalem in Early Islam.* Jerusalem, 2000.

LeStrange, Guy. *Palestine under the Moslems.* London, 1890; repr. Beirut, 1965, and Stanford, 2003. Still indispensable for its use of classical Arabic sources and for the thoroughness of its coverage.

Pahlitsch, Johannes, and Lorenz Korn. *Governing the Holy City.* Wiesbaden, 2004. Scholarly study of mostly written sources.

Peters, Frank E. *The Distant Shrine: The Islamic Centuries in Jerusalem.* New York, 1993. Clear and well written survey.

Prawer, Joshua, and Haggai Ben-Shammai, eds. *The History of Jerusalem:*

The Early Muslim Period, 638–1099. Jerusalem, 1996. A multi-authored scholarly volume which introduces all the components of the history of Jerusalem; excellent "physical strata" by Dan Bahat.

Rosovsky, Nitza. *City of the Great King.* Cambridge, 1996. A compendium of many studies, most of them quite original, about the components of Jerusalem in history.

Van Berchem, Max. *Matériaux pour un Corpus Inscriptionum Arabicarum.* 3 vols. Cairo, 1920–1927; repr. Geneva, 2001. An absolutely essential compendium of basic sources with thoughtful and learned comments.

de Vogüé, Melchior. *Le Temple de Jérusalem.* Paris, 1864. This first significant work on the subject is a sumptuous volume, whose introduction alone deserves to be read and re-read.

Wilkinson, John. *Jerusalem Pilgrims before the Crusades.* Warminster, 1977. Indispensable selection of Christian sources with commentaries.

———. *Jerusalem Pilgrimage, 1099–1185.* London, 1988. Continuation of the preceding.

The Dome of the Rock

Avner, Rita. "The Recovery of the Kathisma Church." In *One Land Many Cultures,* ed. G. Claudio Bottine and others. Jerusalem, 2003.

Bottini, G. Claudio, and others. *Christian Archaeology in the Holy Land.* Jerusalem, 1990. For a study by Y. Magen on another important octagonal building, the church of the Virgin on Mount Gerizim.

Brenk, Beat. "Die Christianisierung des jüdischen Stadtzentrum von Kapernaum." In *Byzantine East, Latin West, Studies in Honor of Kurt Weitzmann,* ed. Doula Mouriki and others. Princeton, 1995. Best introduction to the Capernaum octagon.

Busse, Heribert. "Die arabische Inschriften in und an Felsendom in Jerusalem." In *Das Heilige Land.* 1977.

Chen, Doron. "The Design of the Dome of the Rock in Jerusalem." *Palestine Exploration Quarterly* 112 (1980). Hypothesis about the geometric scheme involved in the construction.

———. "Sir Archibald Creswell's Setting out of the Dome of the Rock." *Palestine Exploration Quarterly* 117 (1985).

Creswell, K. A. C. *Early Muslim Architecture.* 2nd ed. Oxford, 1969; repr. New York, 1978. The chapters devoted to the building and decoration of the Dome of the Rock are the most complete and thorough in existence; the bibliography attached to these chapters is also quite complete.

Ecochard, Michel. *Filiation de Monuments Grecs, Byzantins et Islamiques.* Paris, 1972.

Golombek, Lisa. "The Draped Universe of Islam." In *Content and Context of Visual Arts in the Islamic World,* ed. Priscilla Soucek. University Park, Penn., 1988.

Hmelnitskij, Sergei. "Metricheskaia Sekta v Arhitektury Kubbat as-Sahra." *Biblioteca Turkmenica 1999.* St. Petersburg, 2001. Another metrical analysis of the plan.

Holum, Kenneth G., and others. *Caesarea Papers* 2, Supplemenatry Papers to *Journal of Roman Archaeology* 35 (1999). On the Caesarea octagon.

Johns, Jeremy. *Bayt al-Maqdis, Jerusalem and Early Islam.* Oxford, 1999. Important although less clearly focused on Jerusalem than its predecessor volume, ed. Johns and Raby.

Lavas, Georgios P. "The Kathisma of the Holy Virgin: A Major Shrine." *Deltion, European Center for Byzantine and Post-Byzantine Monuments Newletter* 2 (2001). The archaeological evidence for the church.

Khoury, Nouha. "The Dome of the Rock, the Ka'ba, and Ghumdan." *Muqarnas* 10 (1993).

Mekeel-Matheson, Carolanne. "The Meaning of the Dome of the Rock." *The Islamic Quarterly* 43 (1999). A striking and novel interpretation of the building.

Rabbat, Nasser. "The Meaning of the Umayyad Dome of the Rock." *Muqarnas* 6 (1989).

———. "The Dome of the Rock Revisited." *Muqarnas* 10 (1993).

Raby, Julian, and Jeremy Johns, eds. *Bayt al-Maqdis: Abd al-Malik's Jerusalem.* Oxford, 1992. A superb collection of very novel studies on the building by several scholars.

Rosen-Ayalon, Myriam. *Qedem.* Vol. 28, *The Early Islamic Monuments of al-Haram al-Sharif.* Jerusalem, 1989.

Shamma, Abier Ziadeh. *The Umayyad Dome of the Rock: A Seventh Century Cultural Paradigm.* PhD diss., UCLA, 2004. Original, if not always acceptable, explanation of the building.

Shani, Raya. "The Iconography of the Dome of the Rock." *Jerusalem Studies in Arabic and Islam* 23 (1999).

Soucek, Priscilla. "The Temple of Solomon in Islamic Art." In *The Temple of Solomon,* ed. Joseph Guttman. Ann Arbor, 1976.

Van Ess, Josef. "Abd al-Malik and the Dome of the Rock." In *Bayt al-Maqdis,* ed. Julian Raby. Oxford, 1992.

———. "Vision and Ascension." *Journal of Qur'anic Studies* I (1989).

700–1100

Baer, Eva. "The Mihrab in the Cave of the Dome of the Rock." *Muqarnas* 3 (1985).

Burgoyne, Michael, and Amal Abu'l Hajj. "Twenty-four Medieval Arabic Inscriptions." *Levant* 11 (1979). For the Maqam Ghuri.

Elad, Amikam. "The Historical Value of *al-fada'il al-quds* Literature." *Jerusalem Studies in Arabic and Islam* 14 (1991).

al-Faqih, Ibn. *Abrégé du Livre des pays.* Translated by Henri Massé. Damascus, 1972.

Halm, Heinz. "Der Treuland." *Der Islam* 63 (1986).

Kaplony, Andreas. "Manifestations of Private Piety: Muslims, Christians and Jews in Fatimid Jerusalem." In *Governing the Holy City,* ed. Johannes Pahlitsch and Lorenz Korn. Wiesbaden, 2004.

Milstein, Rachel. "The Evolution of a Visual Motif: The Temple and the Ka'ba." *Israel Oriental Studies* 19 (1999).

al-Maqdisi, Al-Musharraf b. al-Murajja. *Fada'il Bayt al-Maqdis.* Ed. Ofer Livne-Kafri. Shafaram, 1995.

al-Maqdisi, Sharaf al-Din (often spelled al-Muqaddasi). *Ahsan al-Taqasim.* Ed. Michael de Goeje. Leiden, 1906. Partial translation by André Miquel. Damascus, 1963.

Mourad, Suleiman A. "A Note on the Origins of *fada'il bayt al-maqdis* Compilations." *Al-Abhath* 44 (1998).

al-Wasiti, Muhammad b. Ahmad. *Fada'il al-Bayt al-Muqaddas.* Ed. Ofer Livne-Kafri. Jerusalem, 1979.

Crusades

Boas, Adrian J. *Jerusalem in the Time of the Crusades.* London, 2001.

Folda, Jaroslav. *The Art of the Crusaders in the Holy Land.* Cambridge, 1995.

Hoffman, Eva. "Christian Islamic Encounters." *Gesta* 43 (2004).

Meri, Josef W. *Ali al-Harawi's Kitab al-Isharat.* Princeton, 2004.

Muratova, Xenia. "Western Chronicles of the First Crusade." In *Cruasder Art in the Twelfth Century,* ed. Jaroslav Folda. Oxford, 1982. Deals, among other things, with the alleged statue of Muhammad.

Schein, Sylvia. "Between Mount Moriah and the Holy Sepulcher." *Traditio* 40 (1984).

Strzygowski, Joseph. "Ruins of Tombs of Latin Kings on the Haram in Jerusalem." *Speculum* 11 (1936).

Tobler, Titus, ed. *Descriptiones Terrae Sanctae.* Leipzig, 1874.

William of Tyre, *Chronique du Royaume Franc de Jérusalem de 1095 à 1184.* Paris, 1994.

Ayyubids

Aksoy, Sule, and Rachel Milstein. "A Collection of 13th Century Illustrated Hajj Certificates." In *M. Ugur Dermas Armajani,* ed. Ervin Schick. Istanbul, 2000.

Korn, Lorenz, and Johannes Pahlitsch, eds. *Governing the Holy City.* Wiesbaden, 2004.

Rosen-Ayalon, Miriam. "Art and Architecture in Ayyubid Jerusalem." *Israel Exploration Journal* 40 (1990).

———. "Jewish Substratum, Christian History, and Muslim Symbolism." In *The Real and Ideal Jerusalem in Jewish, Christian and Islamic Art,* ed. Bianca Kuhnel. Jerusalem, 1998.

———. "An Ayyubid Inscription in the Dome of the Rock." *Eretz Israel* 20 (1998).

Sourdel-Thomine, Janine. "Une image musulmane de Jérusalem au début du XIIIème siècle." In *Jerusalem, Rome, Constantinople,* ed. Daniel Poirion. Paris, n.d.

Mamluks

Burgoyne, Michael, and others. *Mamluk Jerusalem.* Buckhurst Hill, 1987. First-rate survey of all the monuments of the city and their cultural and historical context.

al-Ulaymi, Mujir al-Din. *Al-Uns al-Jalil fi Ta'rikh al-Quds was al-Khalil.* Amman, 1973. Partial translation by Henri Sauvaire in *Histoire de Jérusalem et d'Hébron.* Paris, 1876.

Taragan, Hana. "The Image of the Dome of the Rock in Cairene Mamluk Architecture." In *The Real and Ideal Jerusalem,* ed. Bianca Kuhnel. Jerusalem, 1998.

Ottomans

Akkach, Samer. "The Poetics of Concealment: Al-Nabulusi's Encounter with the Dome of the Rock." *Muqarnas* 22 (2005).

Auld, Sylvia, and Robert Hillenbrand. *Ottoman Jerusalem: The Living City, 1517–1917.* London, 2000. Two magnificent and indispensable volumes with many illustrations and scholarly discussions varying in completeness and quality on many topics.

Perlmann, Moshe. "A Seventeenth Century Exhortation Concerning al-Aqsa." *Israel Oriental Studies* 3 (1973).

St. Laurent, Beatrice, and Andras Riedlmayer. "Restorations of Jerusalem and the Dome of the Rock and their Political Significance, 1537–1928." *Muqarnas* 10 (1993).

Index